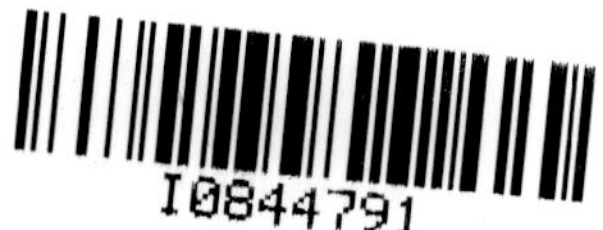

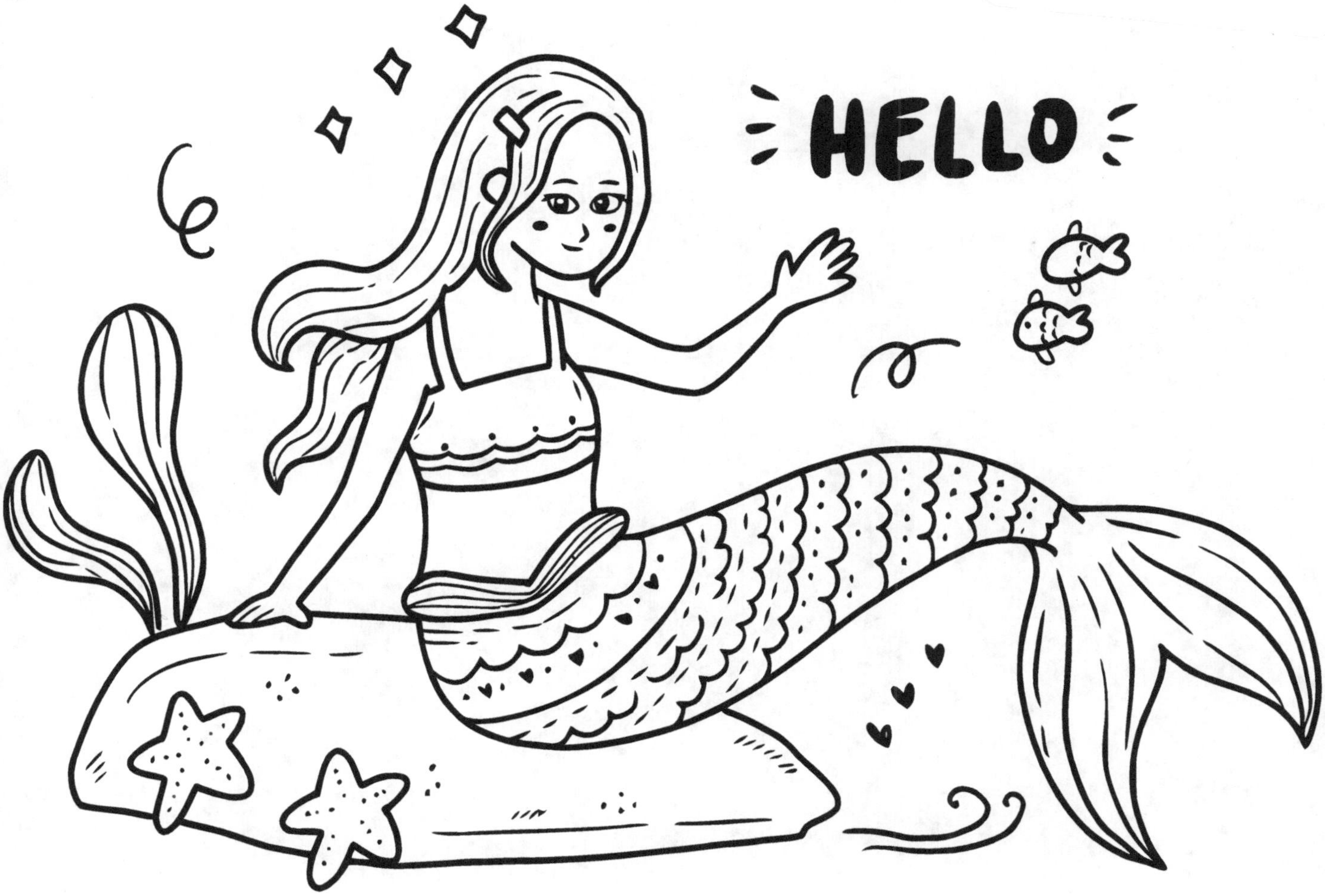

BELONGS TO

____

For any inquiries or questions regarding our books,
please contact us at : jdroyskypublishing@gmail.com

ISBN: 9798533325066

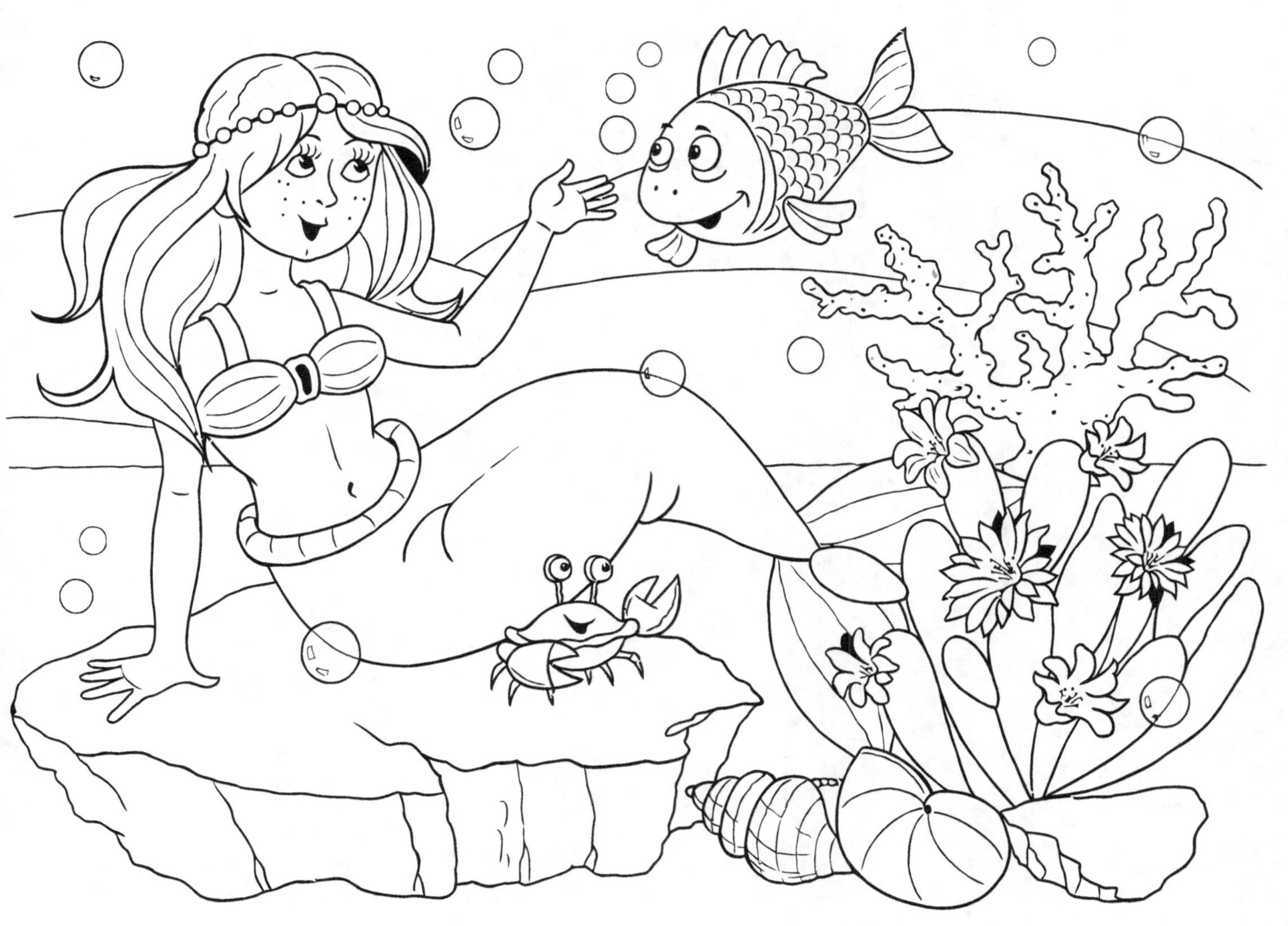

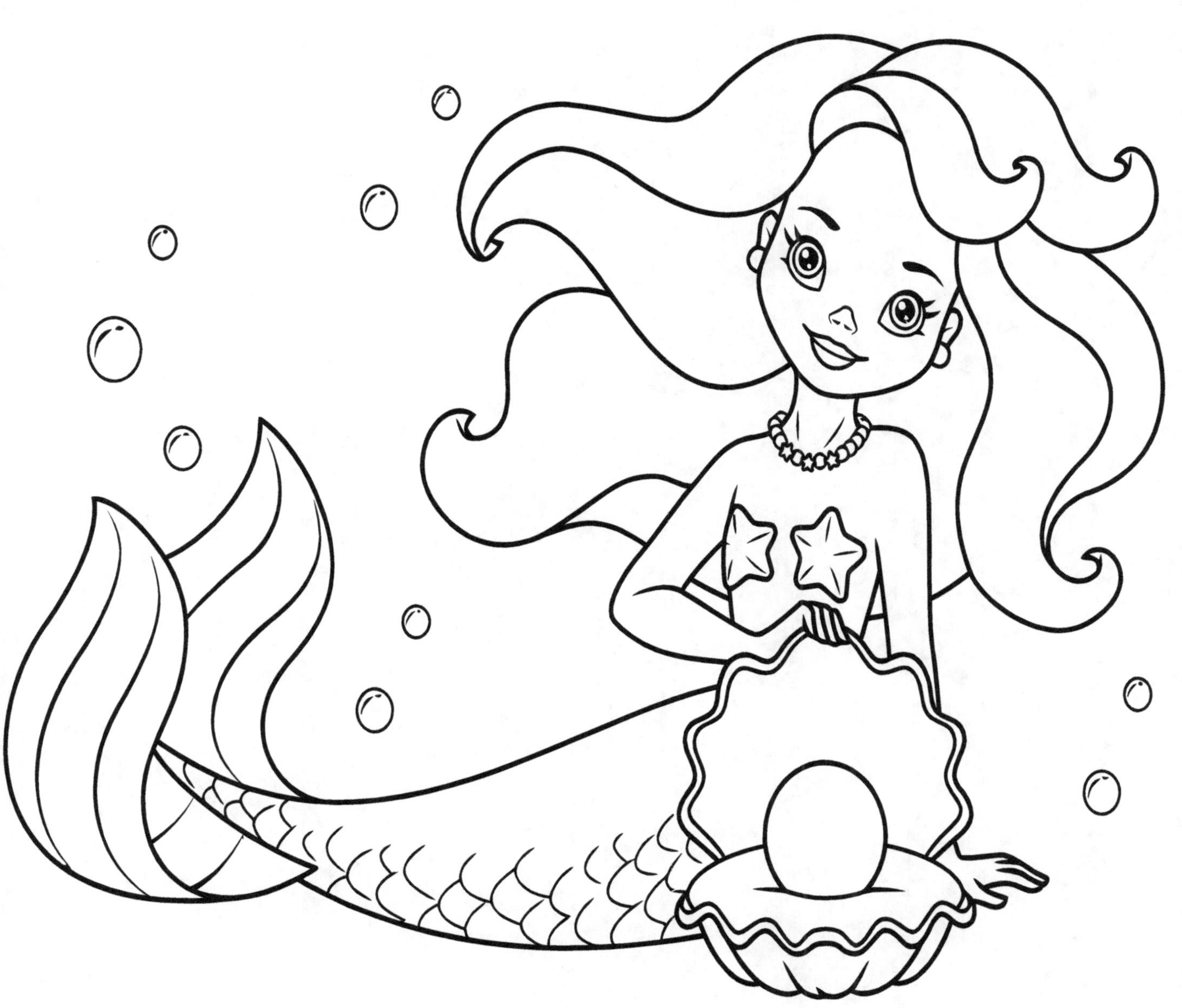

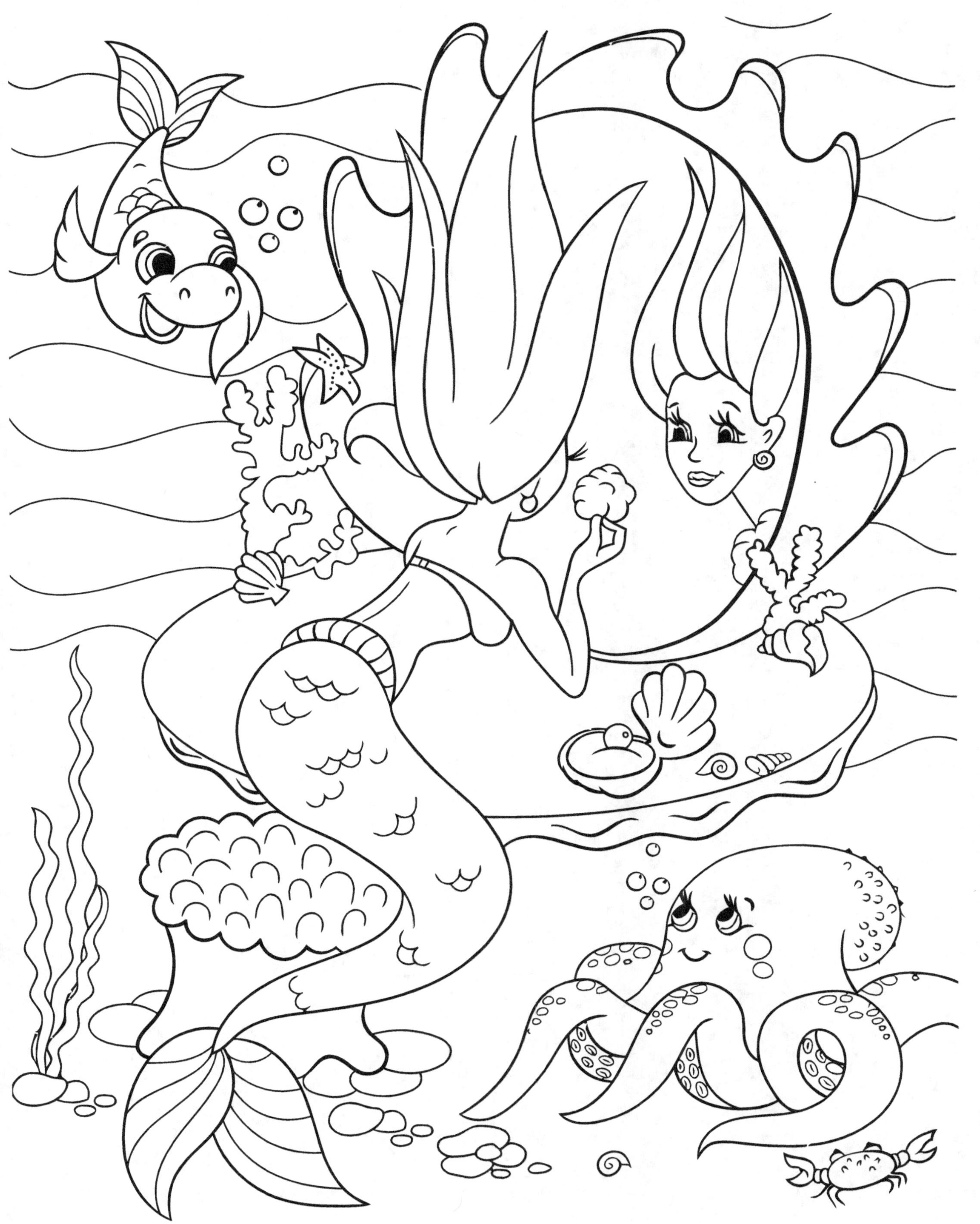

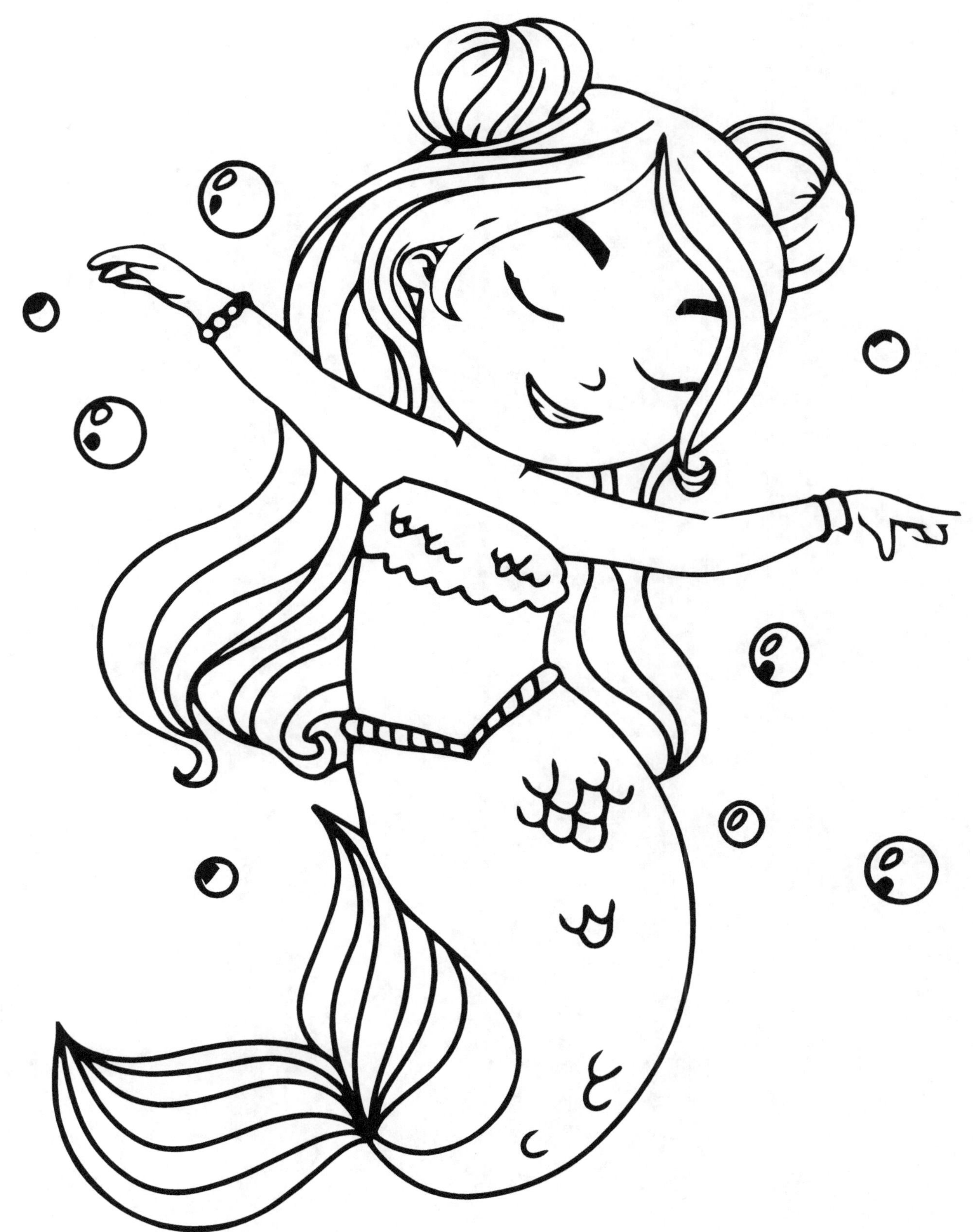

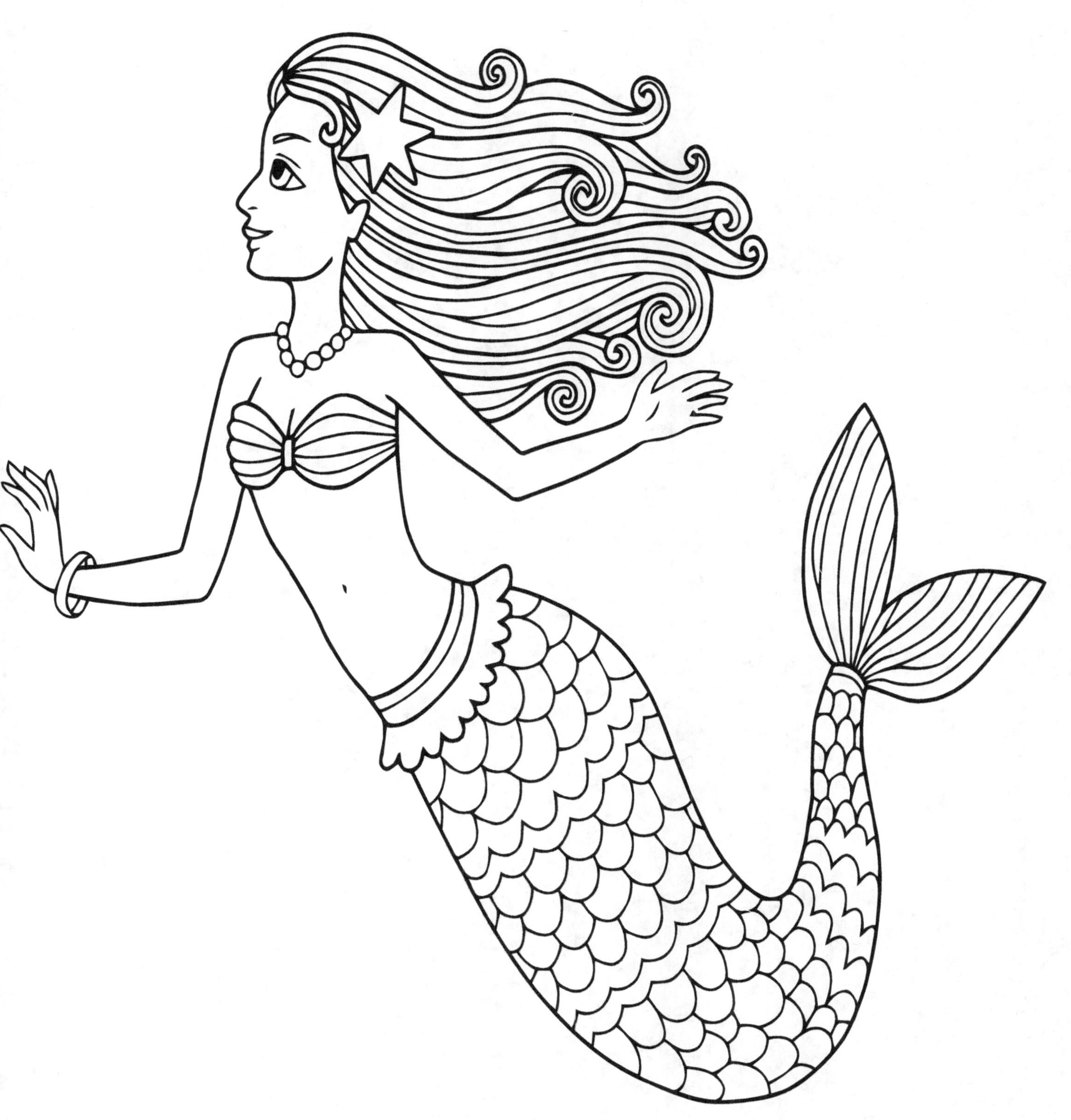

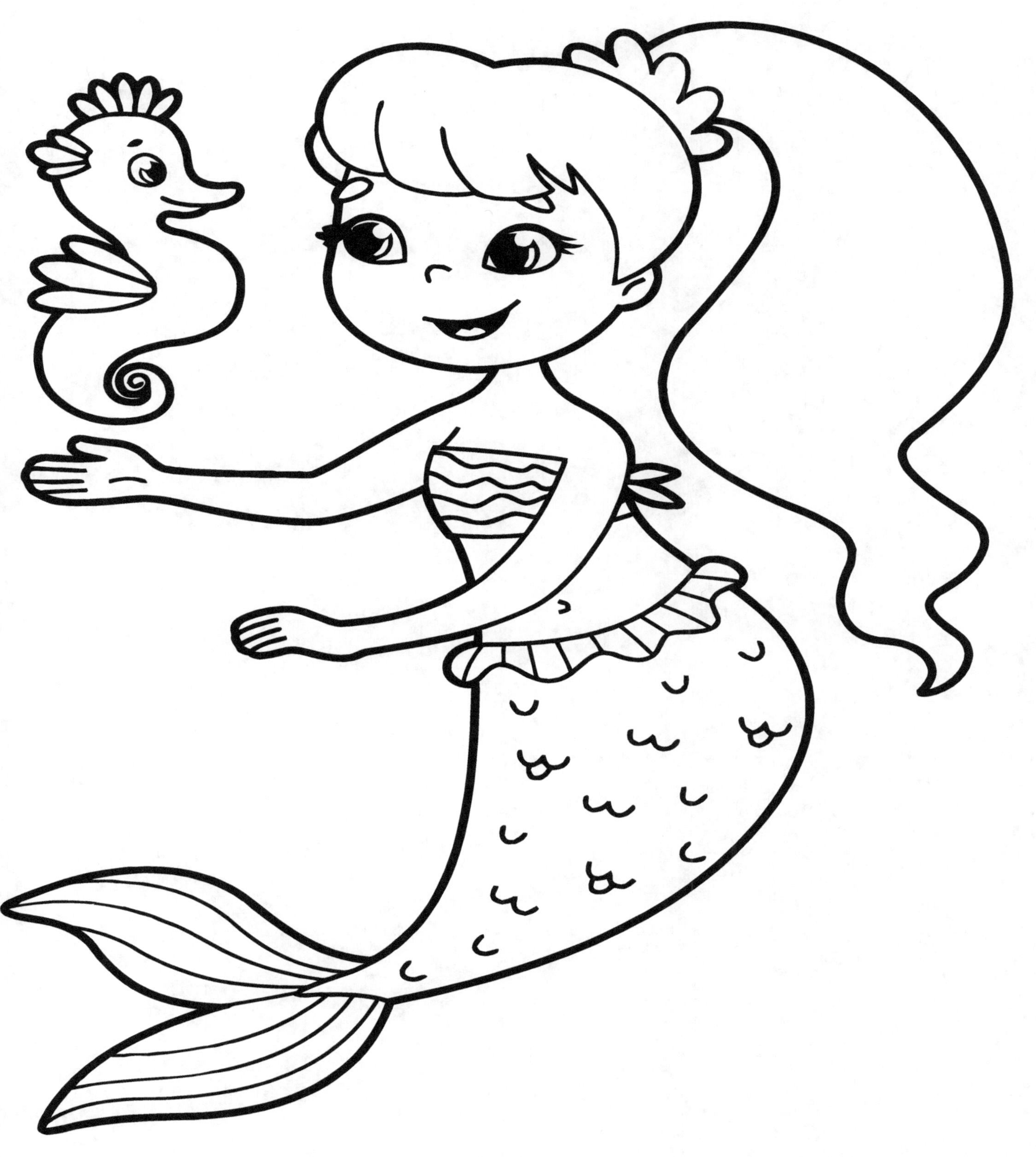

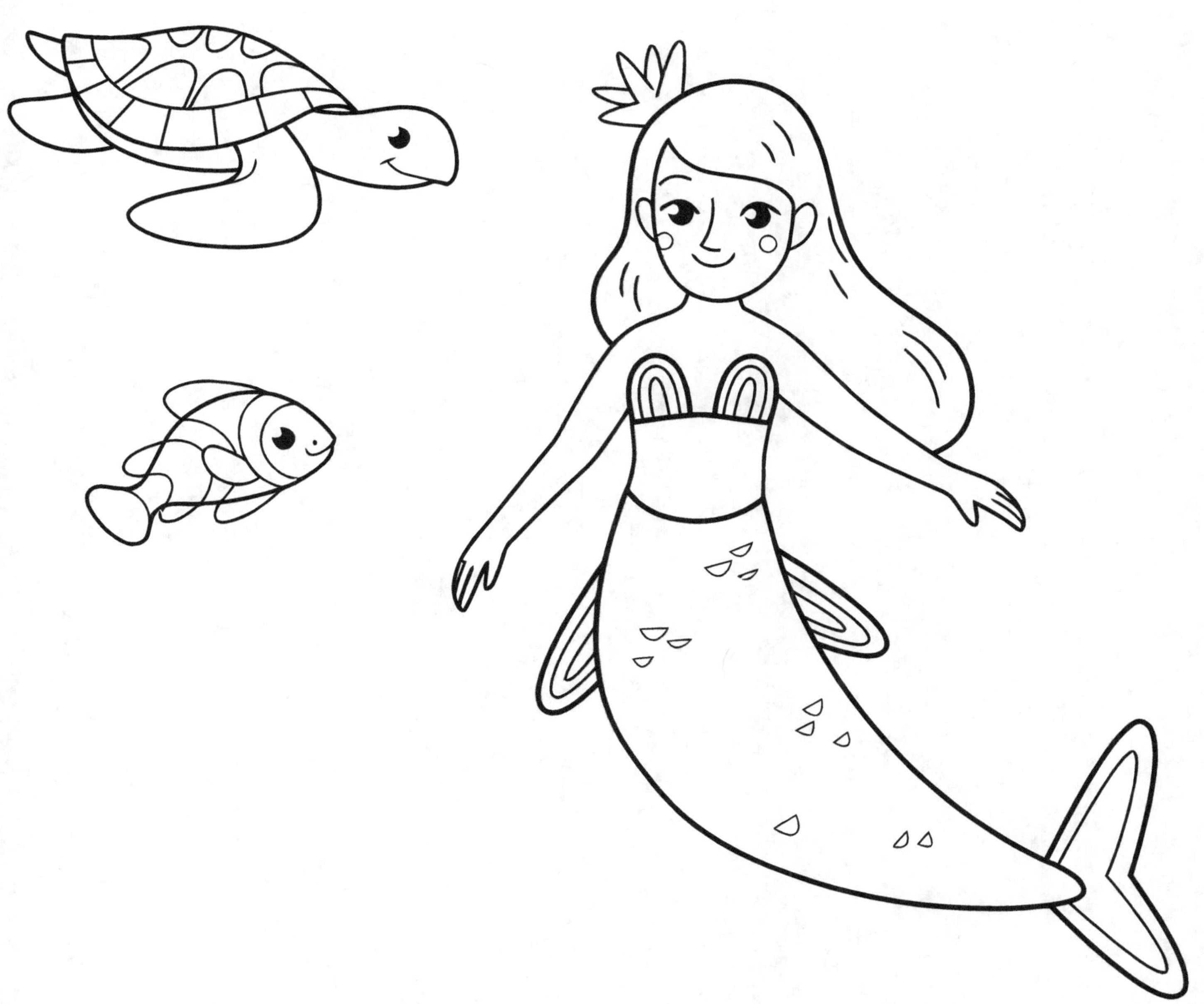

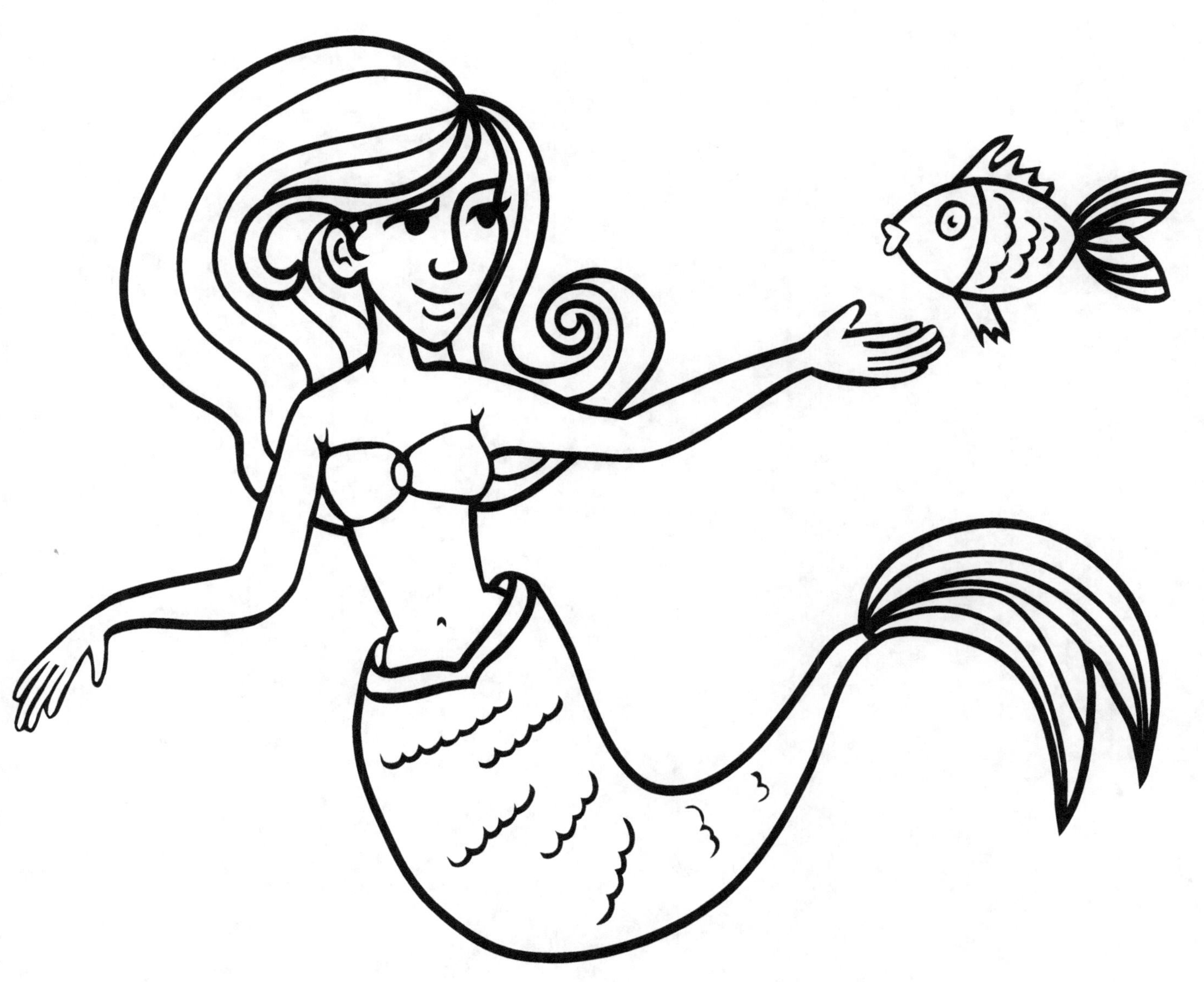

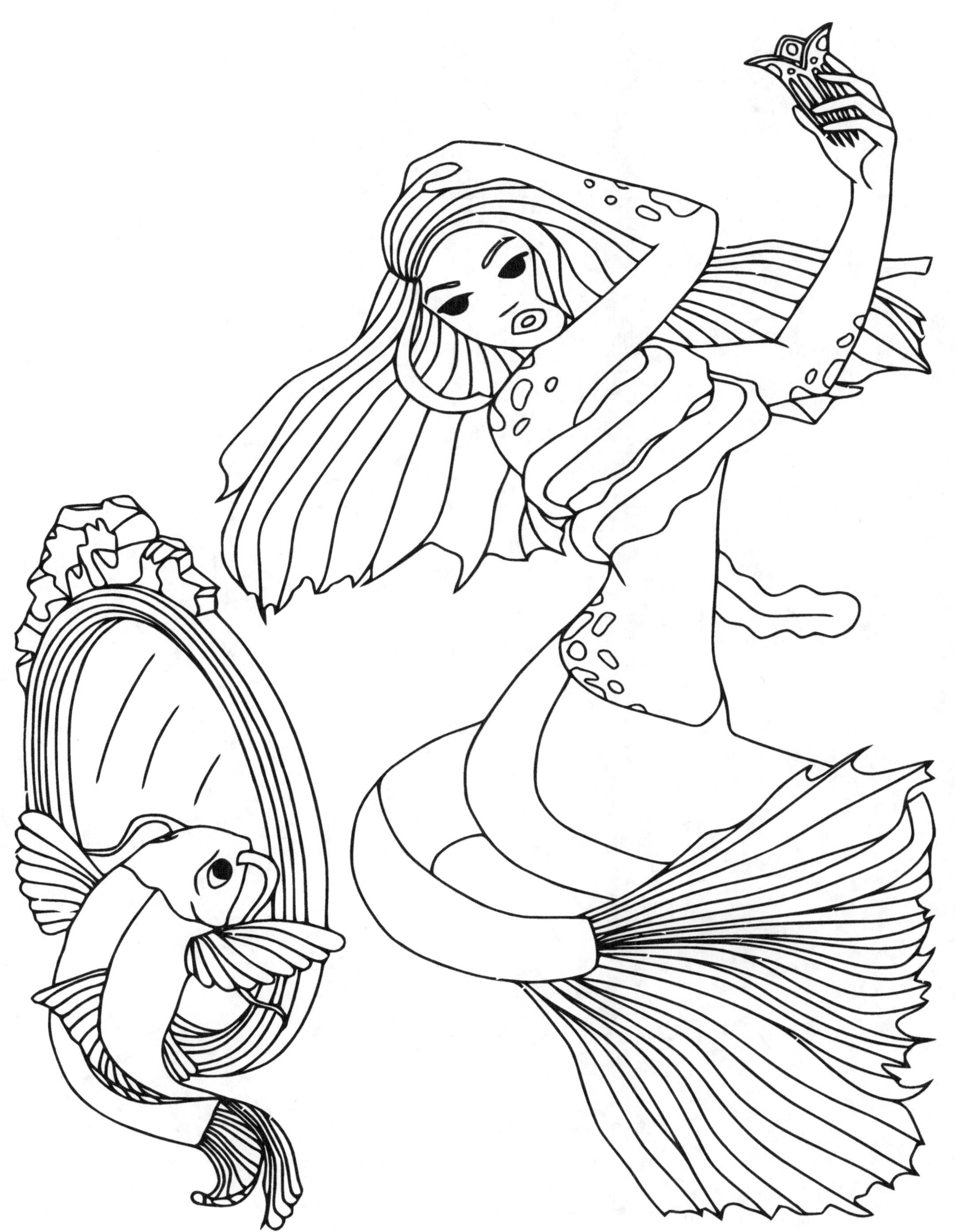

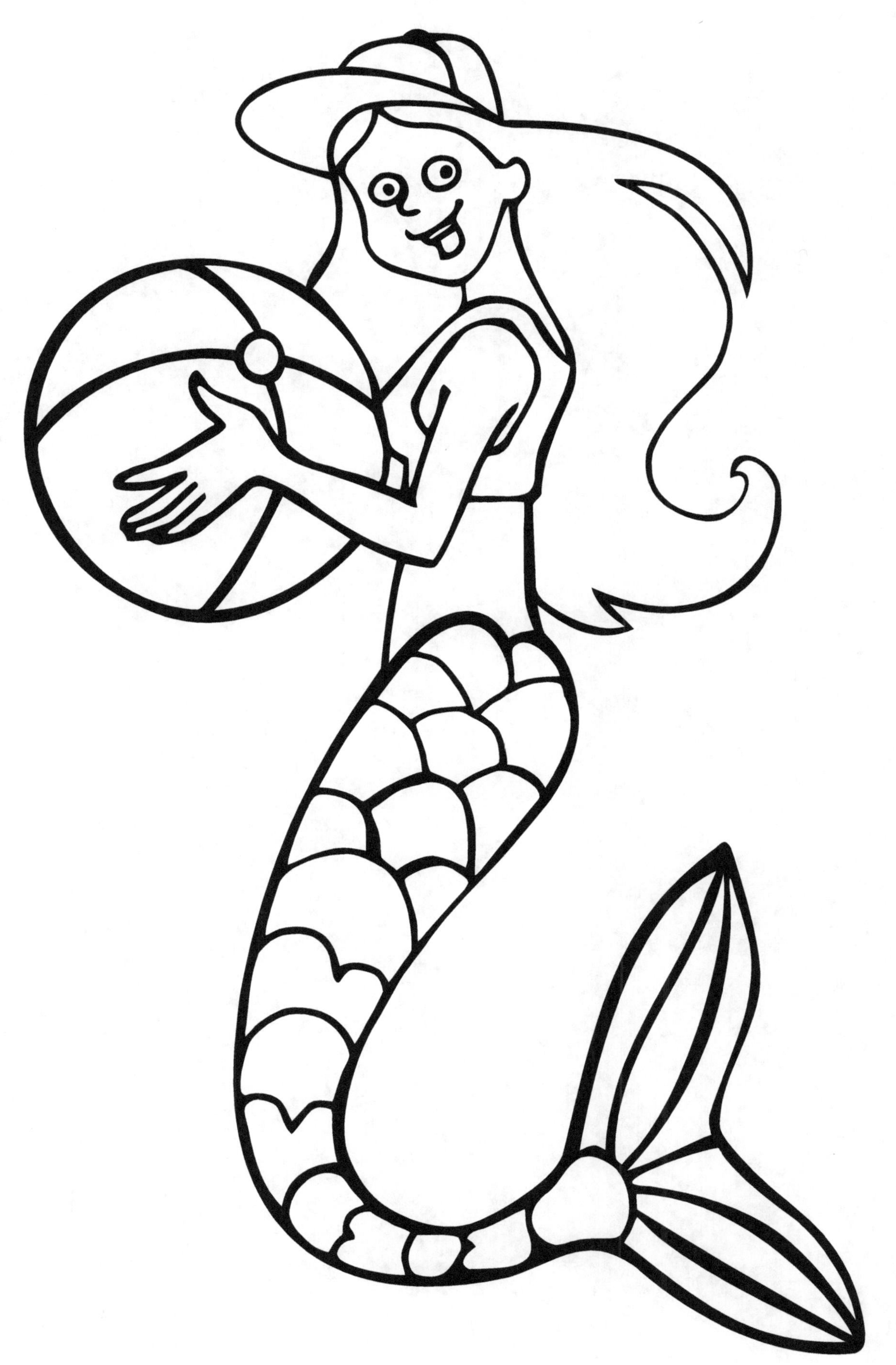

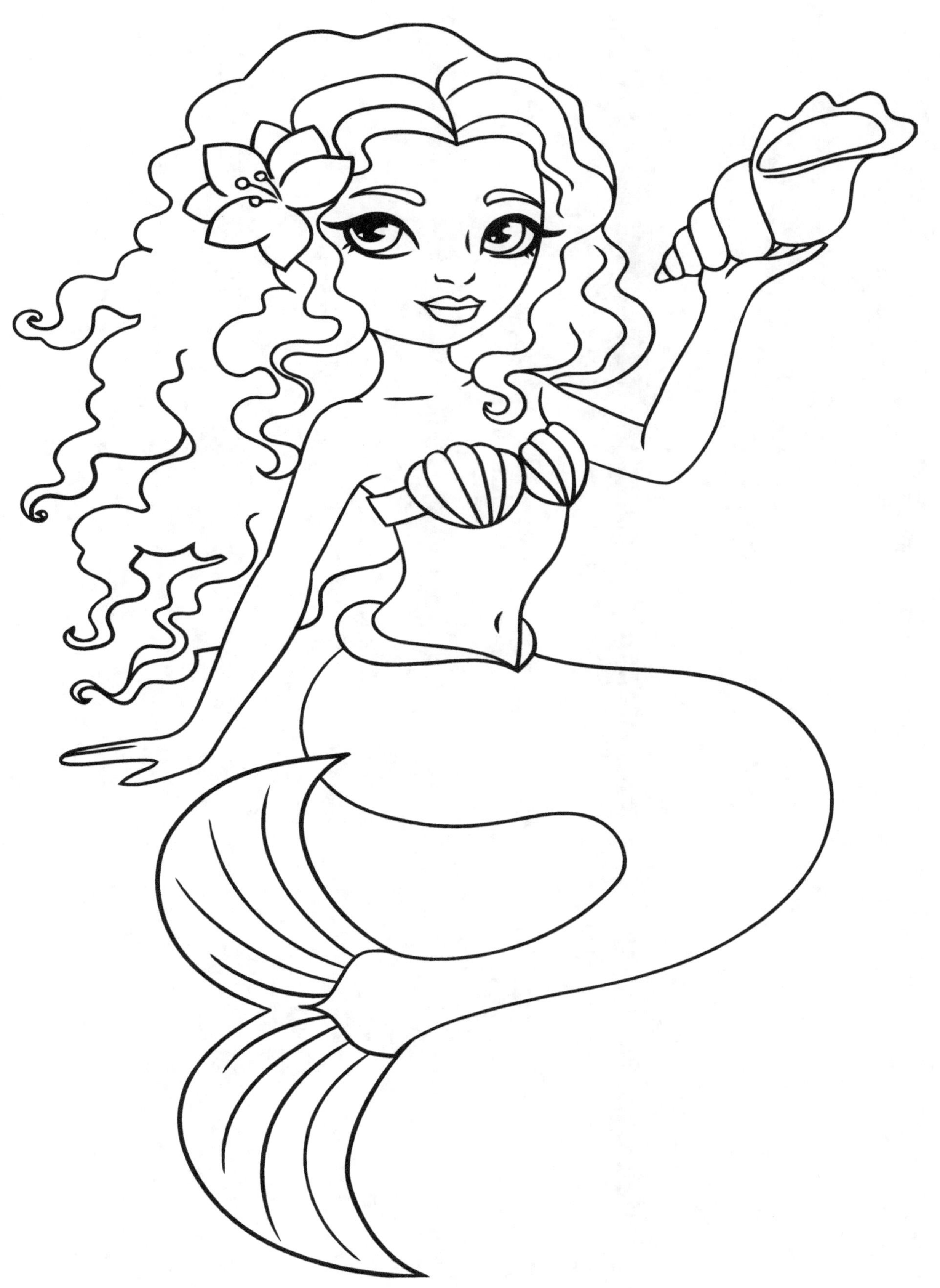

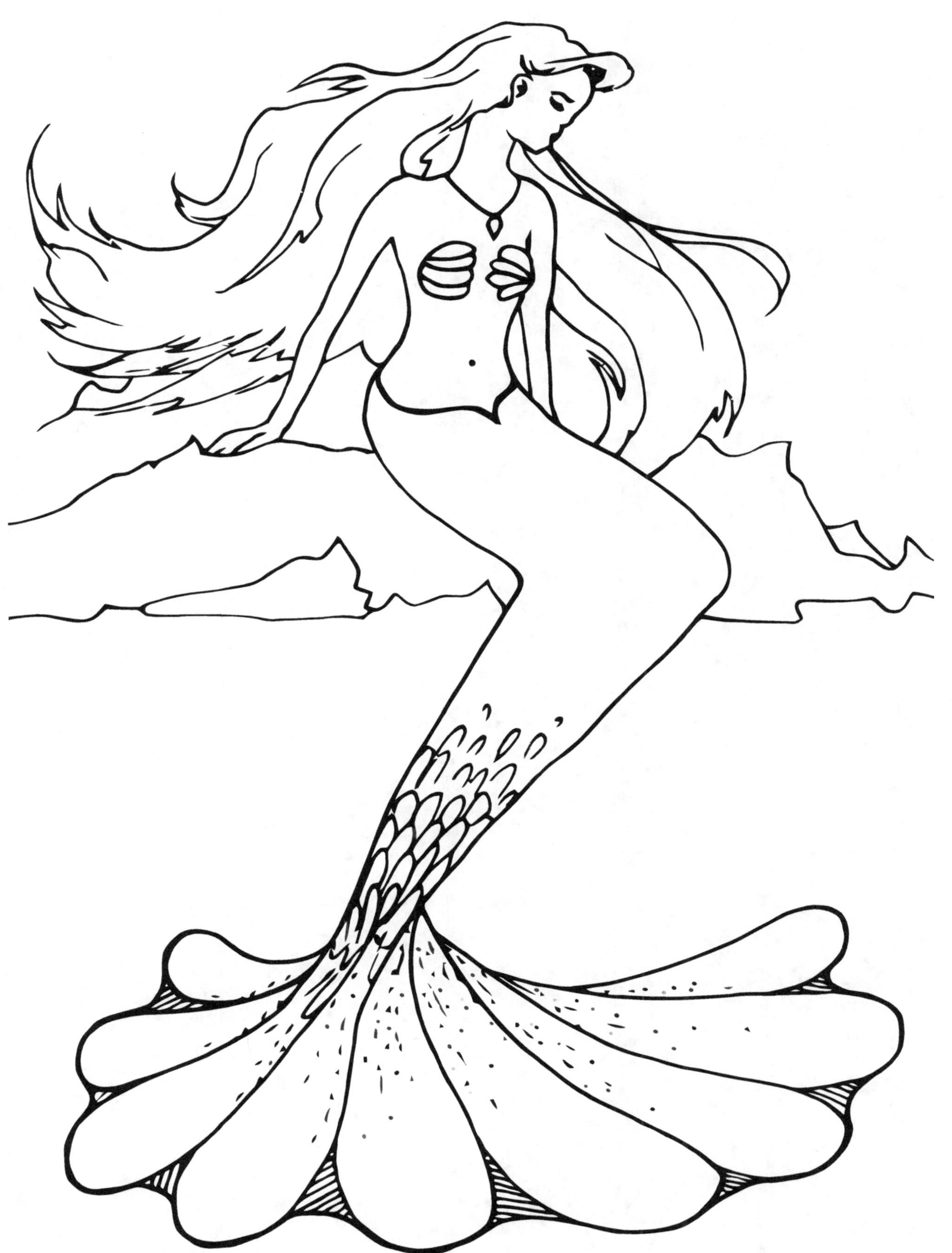

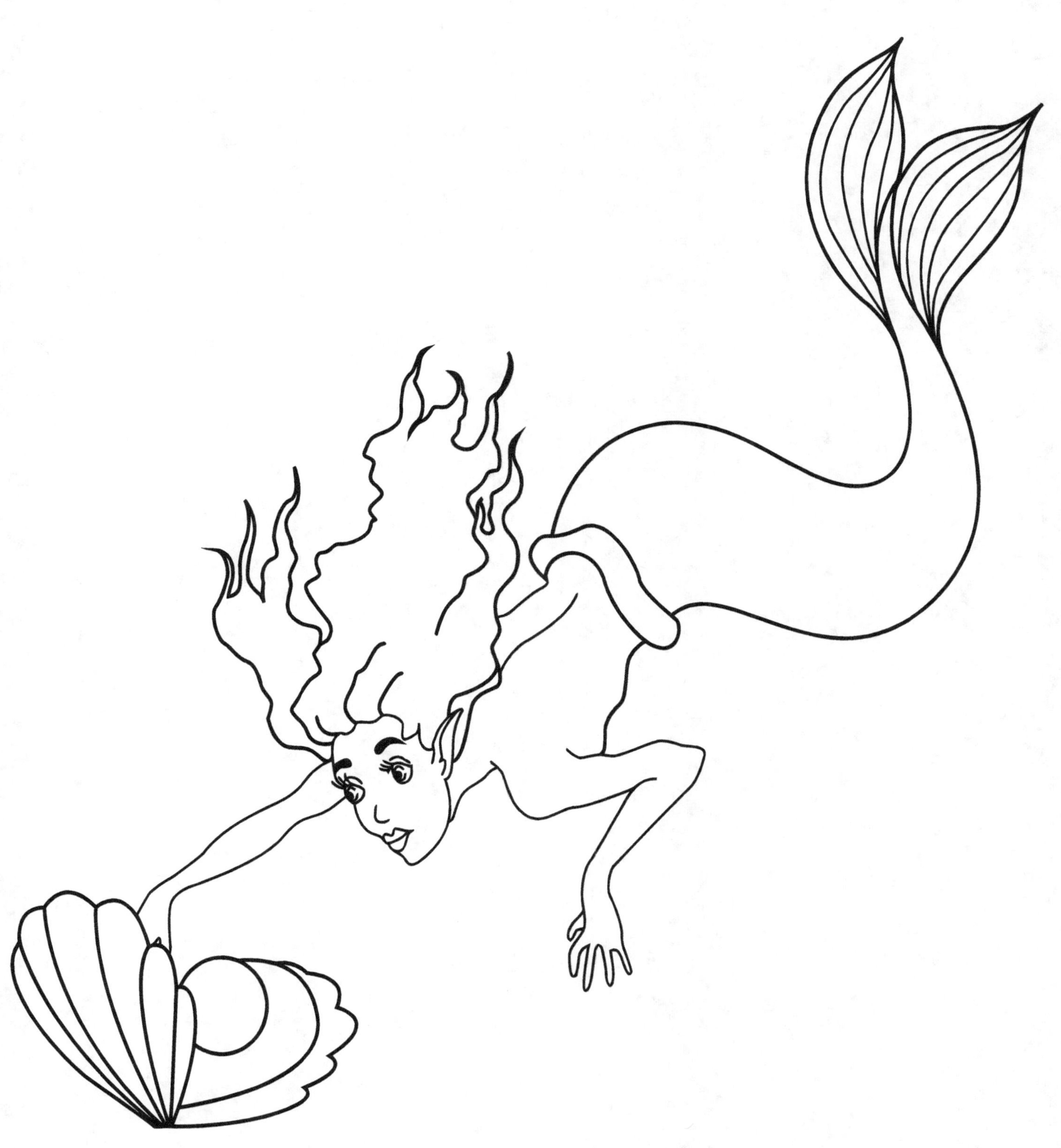

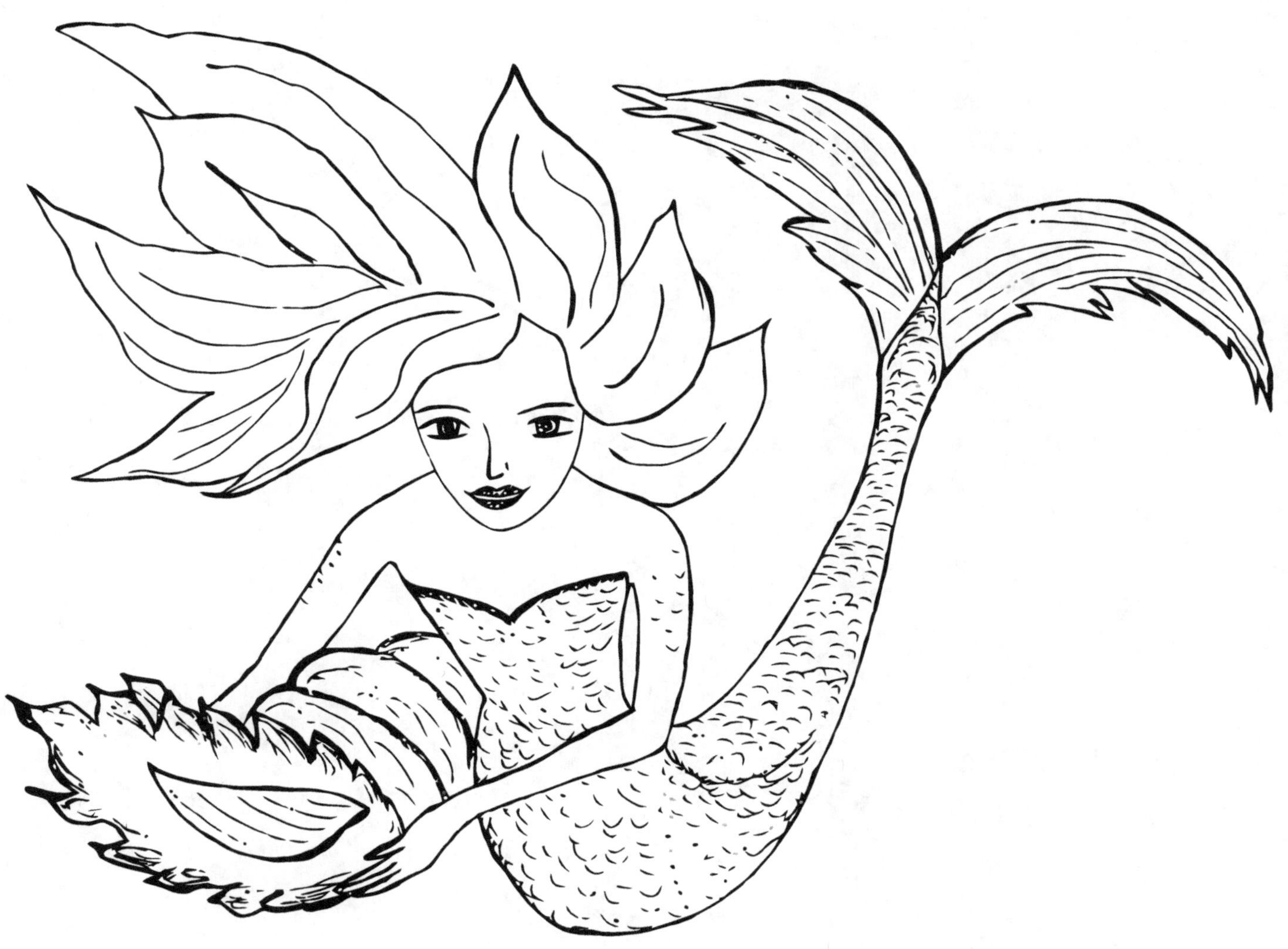

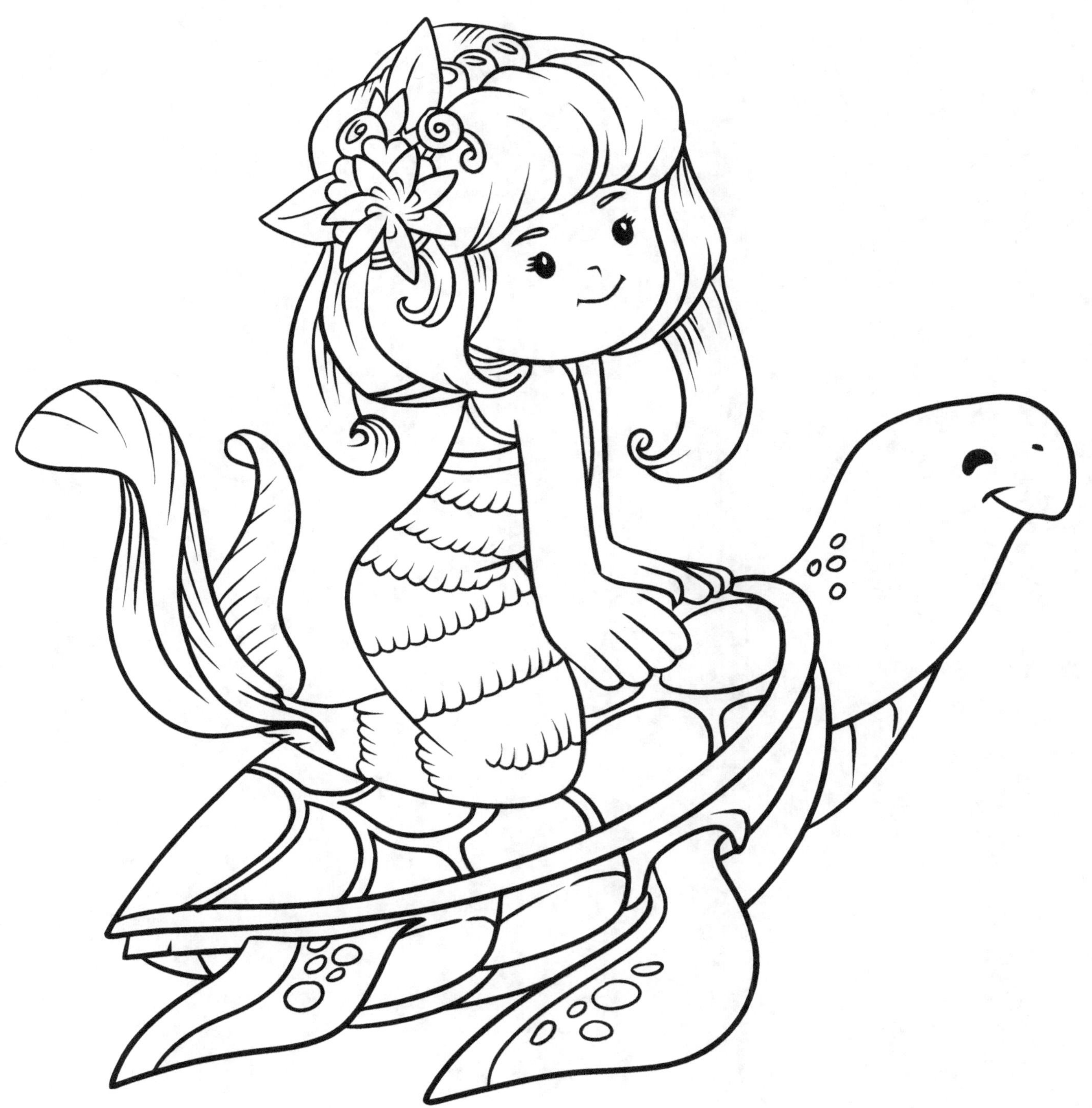

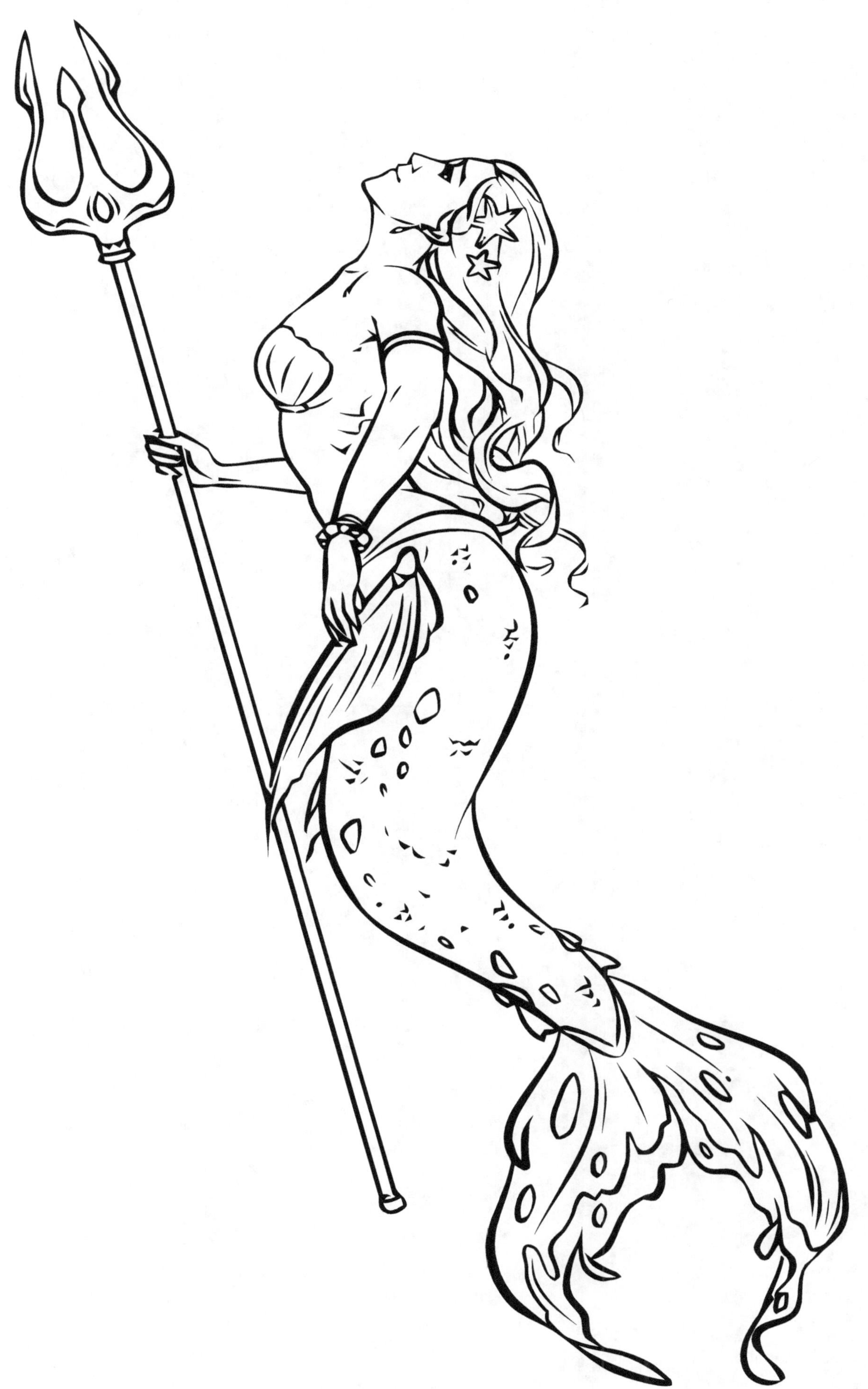

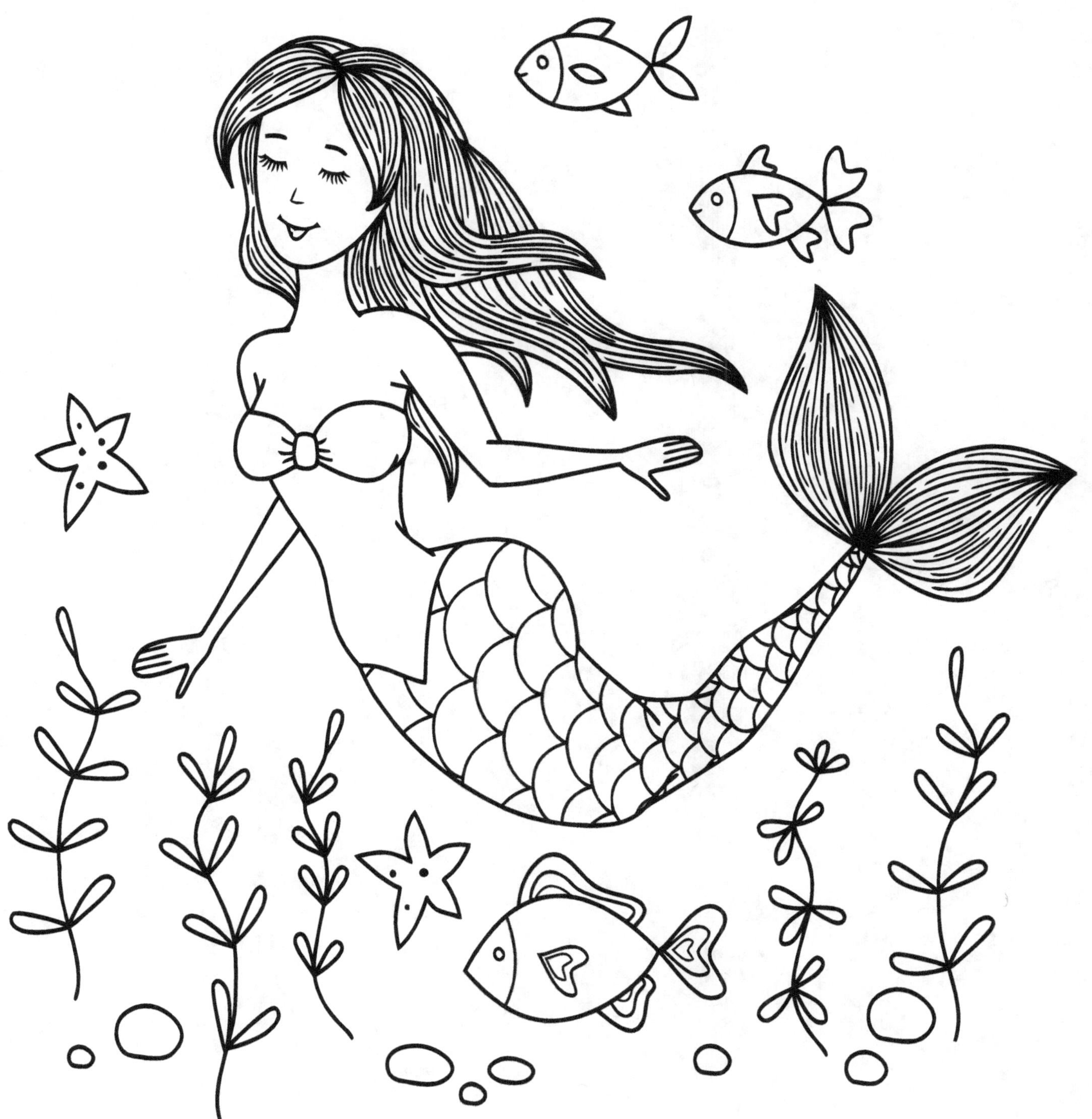

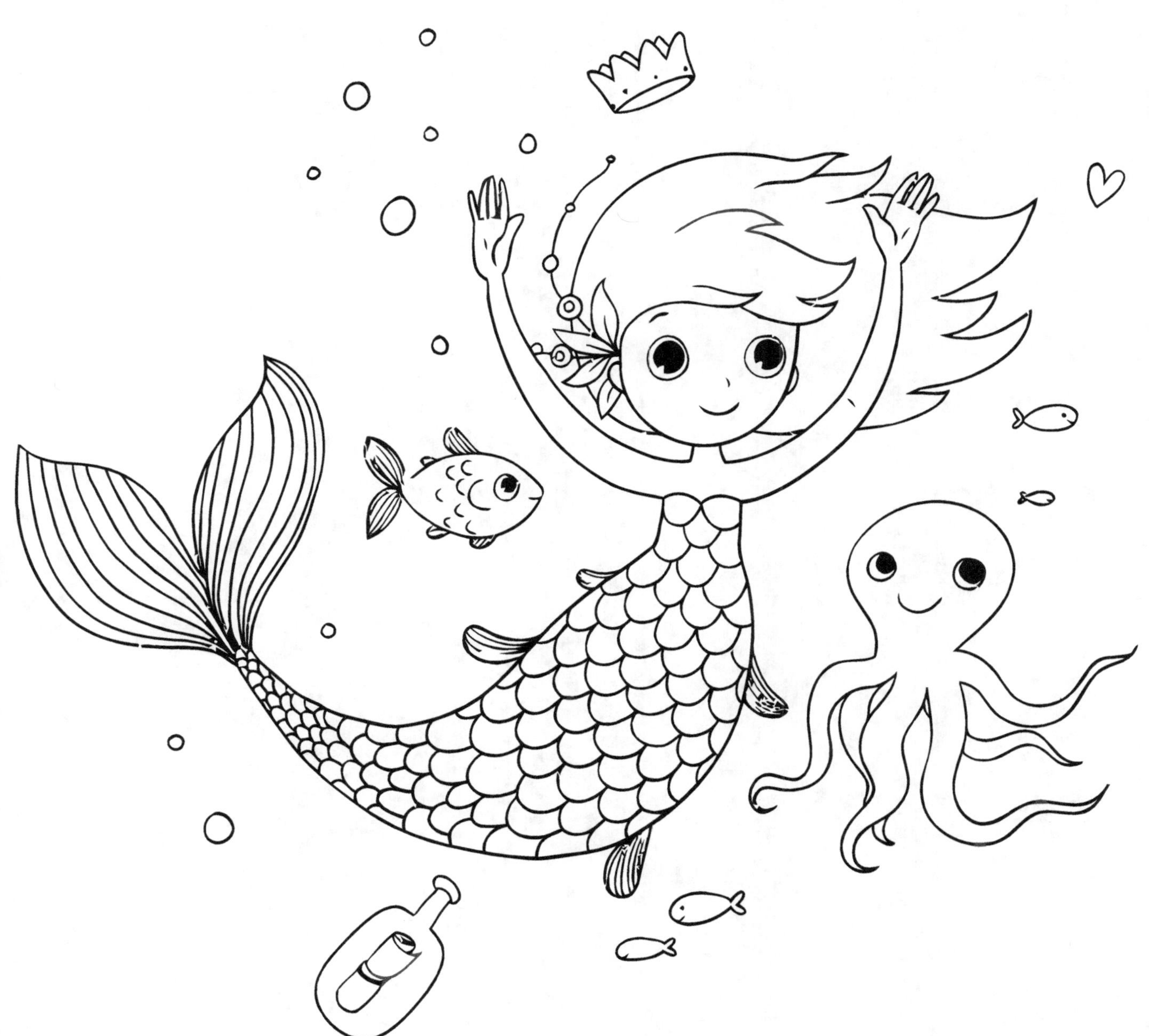

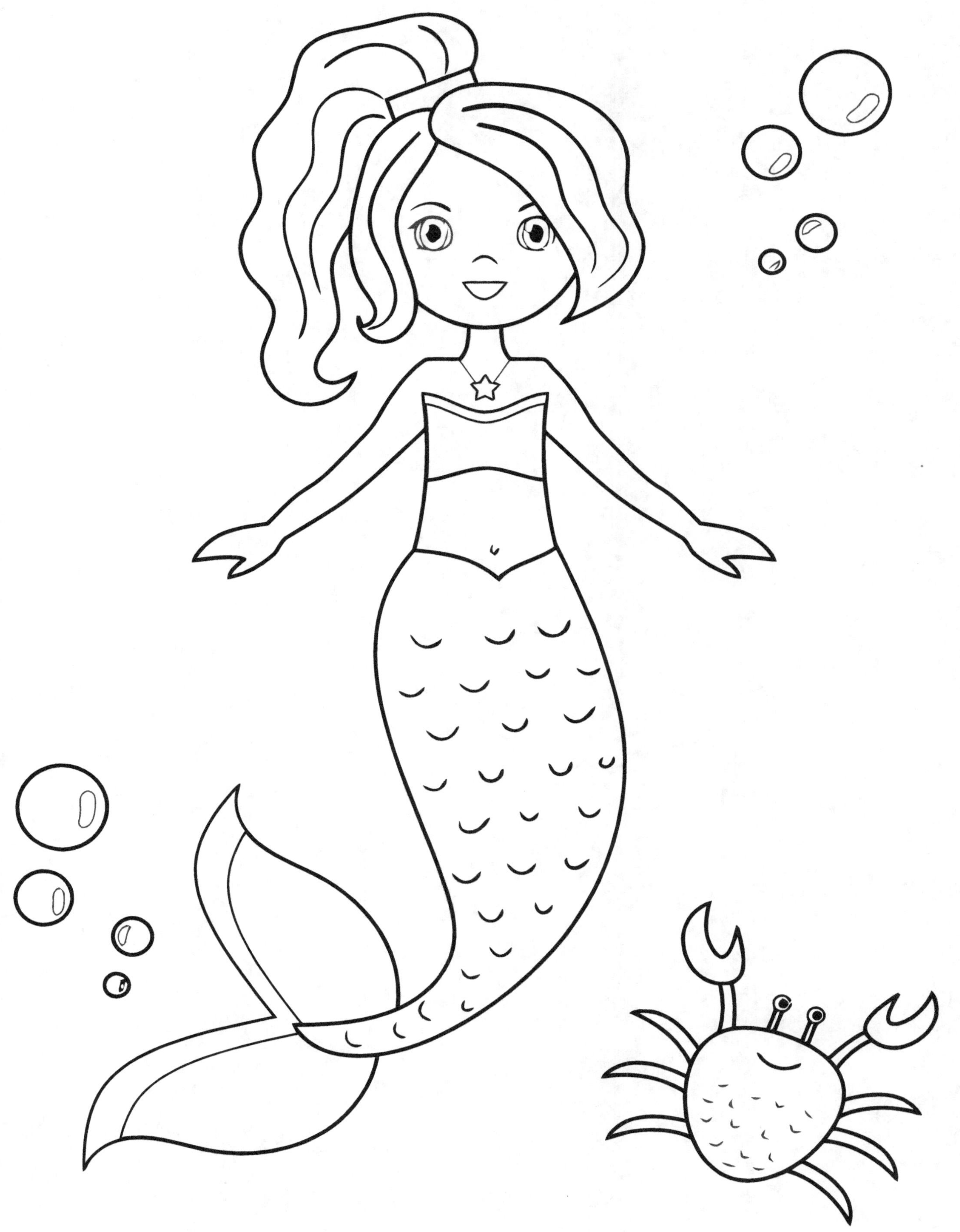

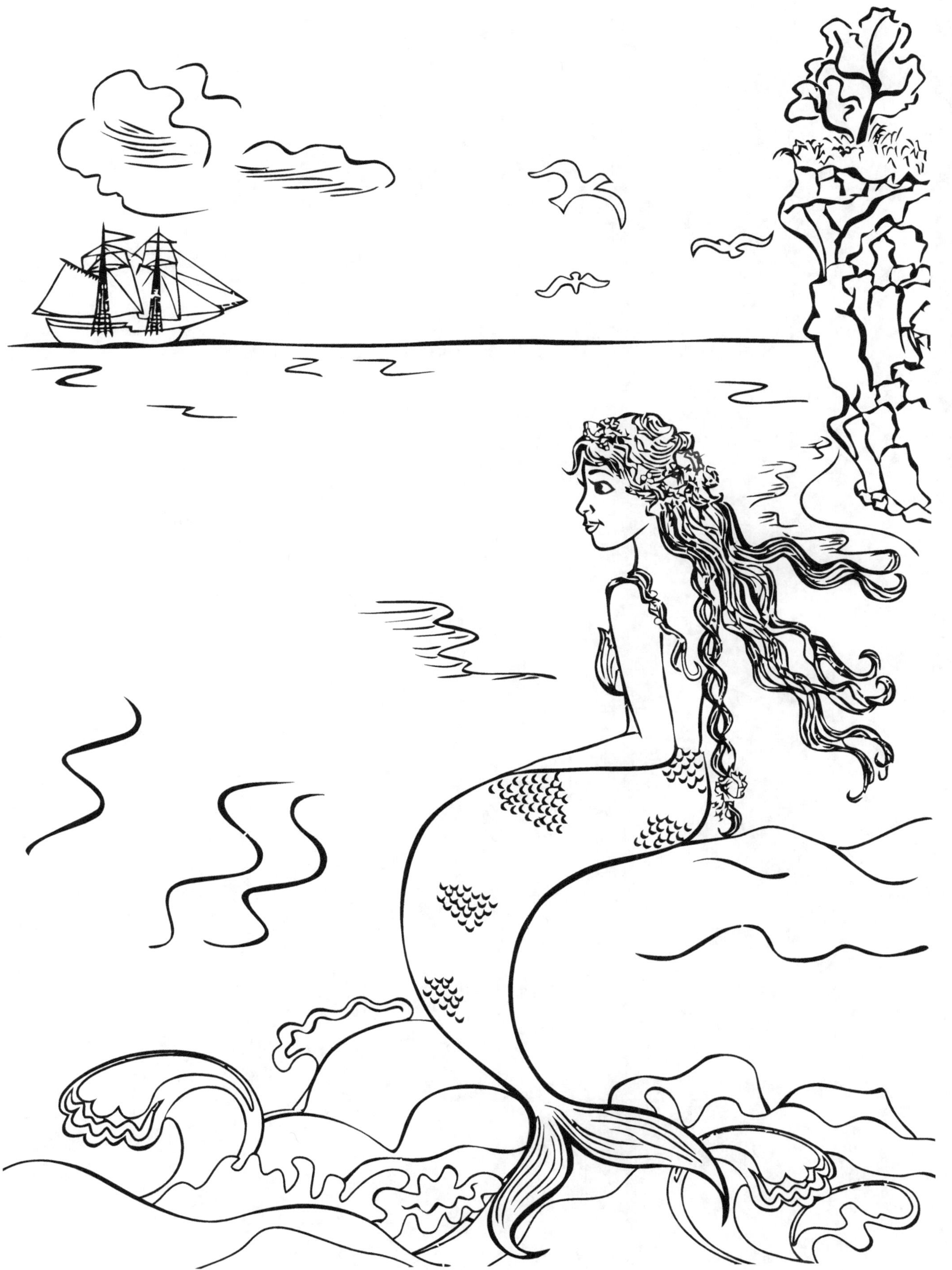

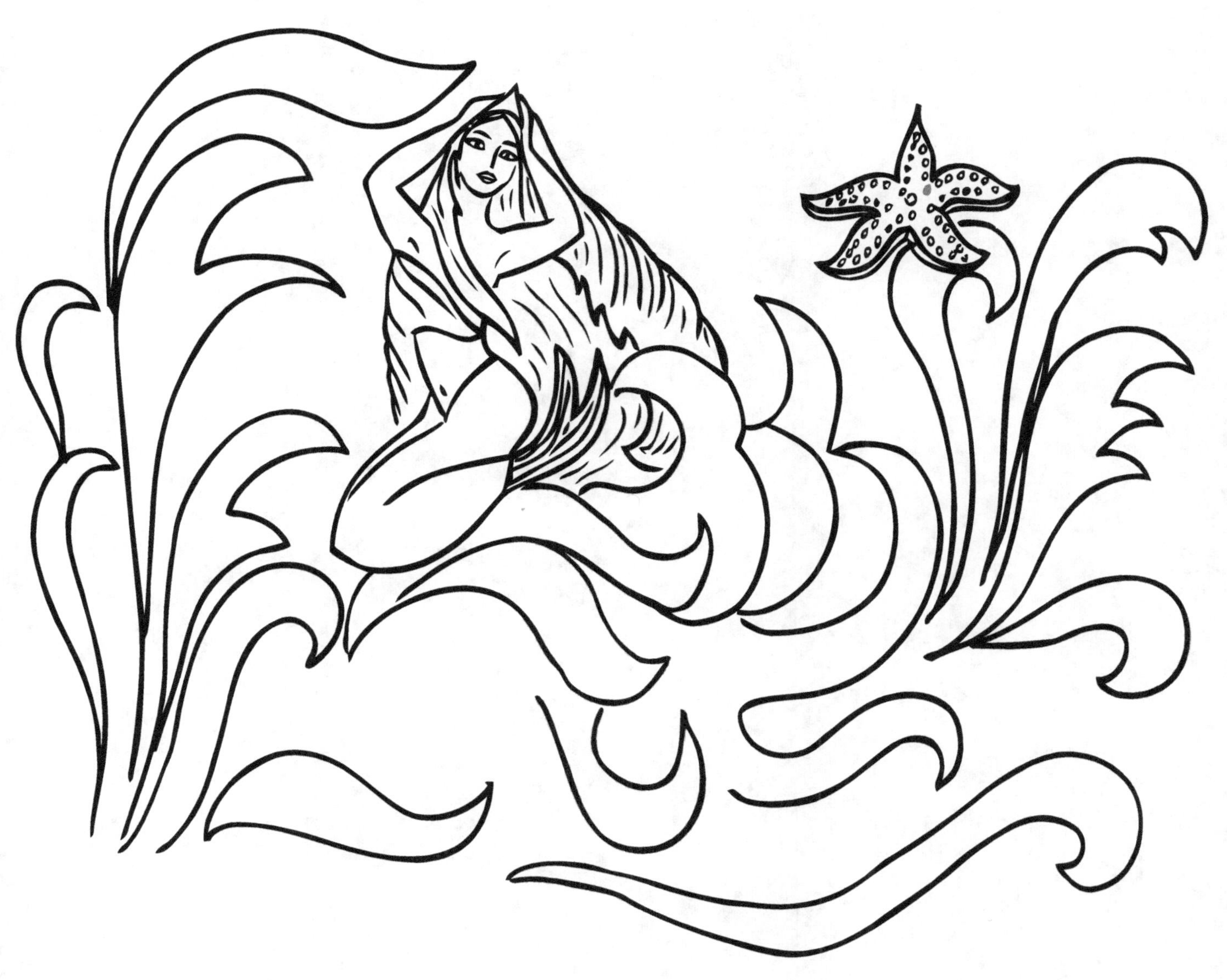

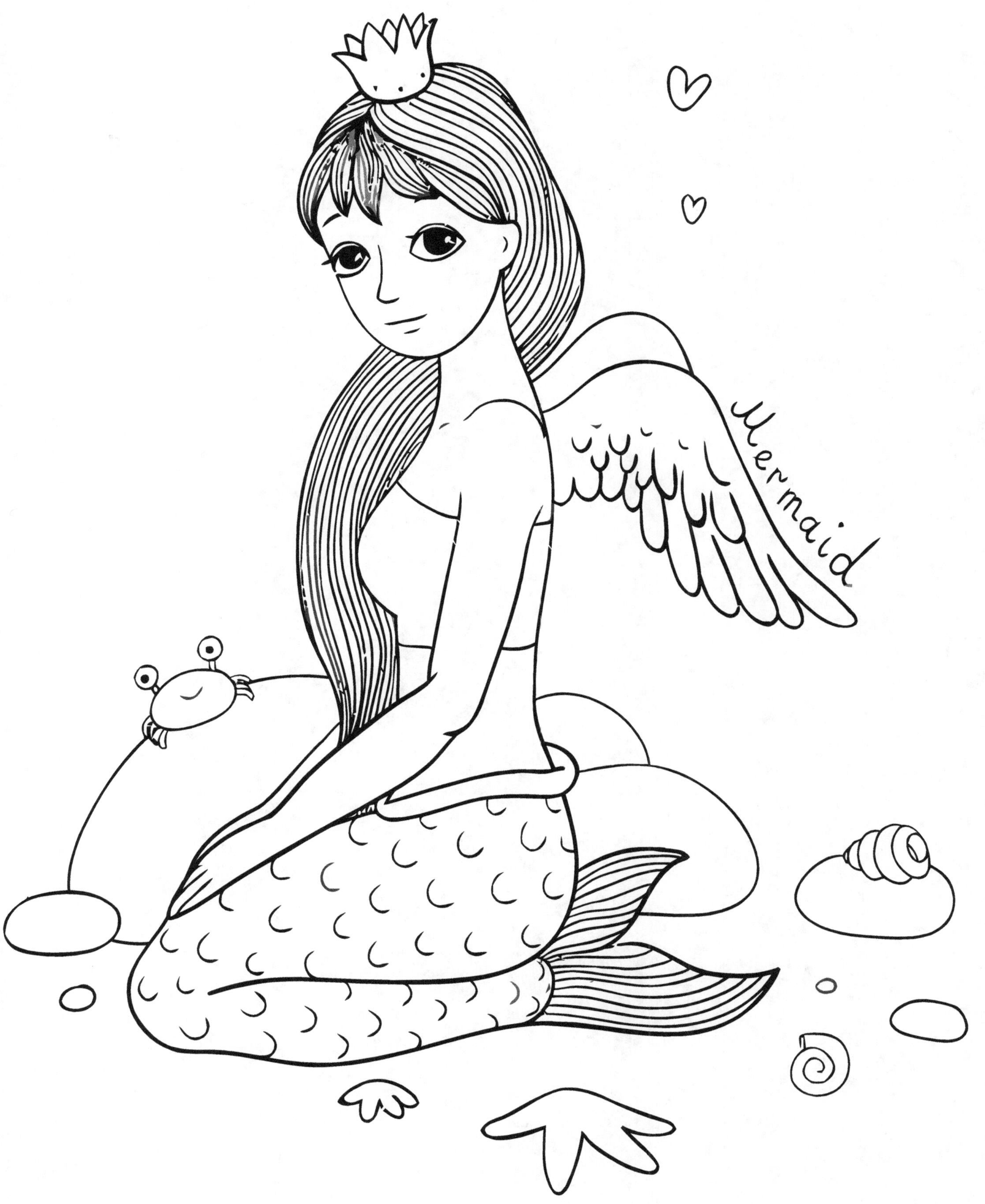

Mermaid

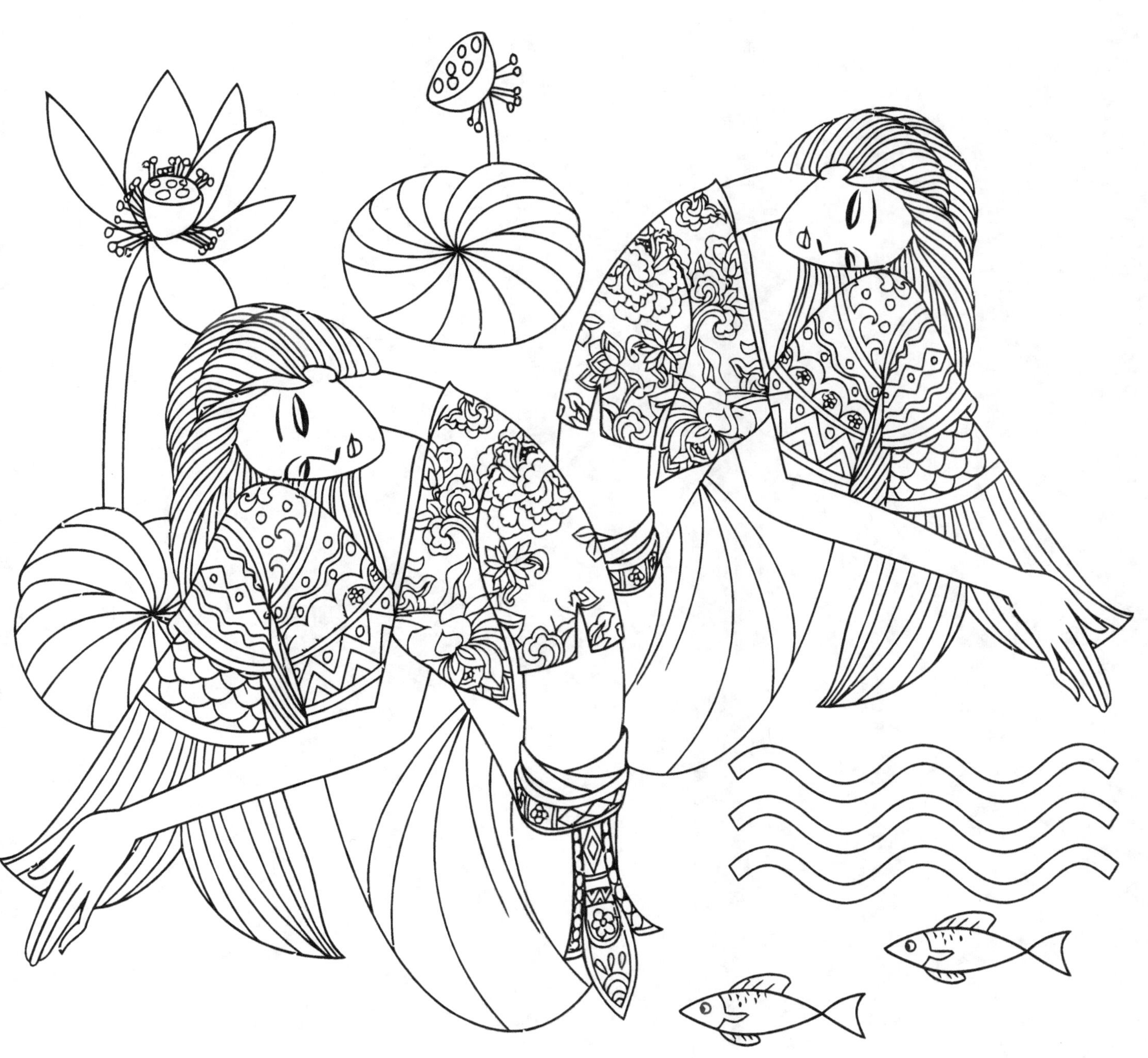

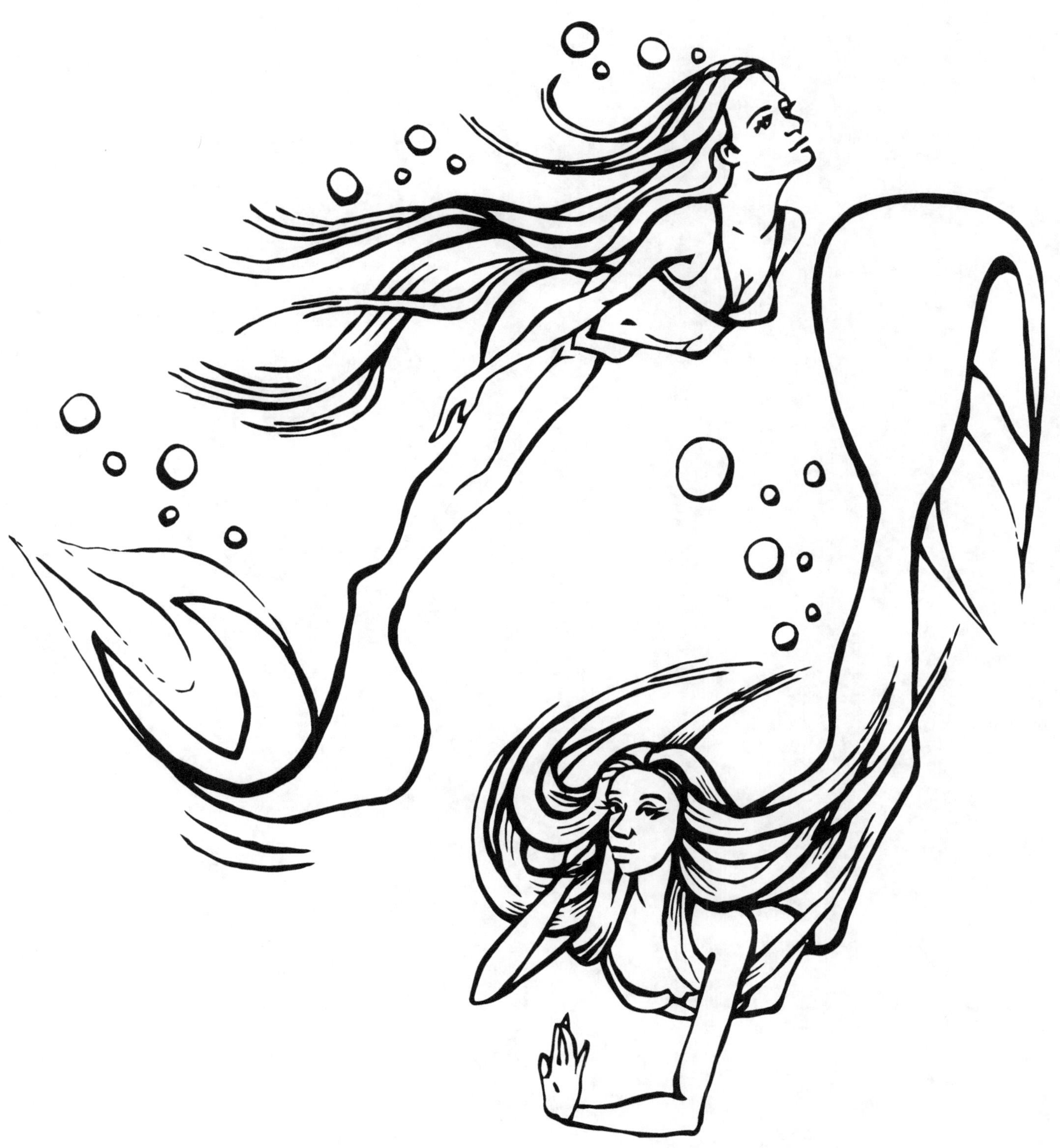

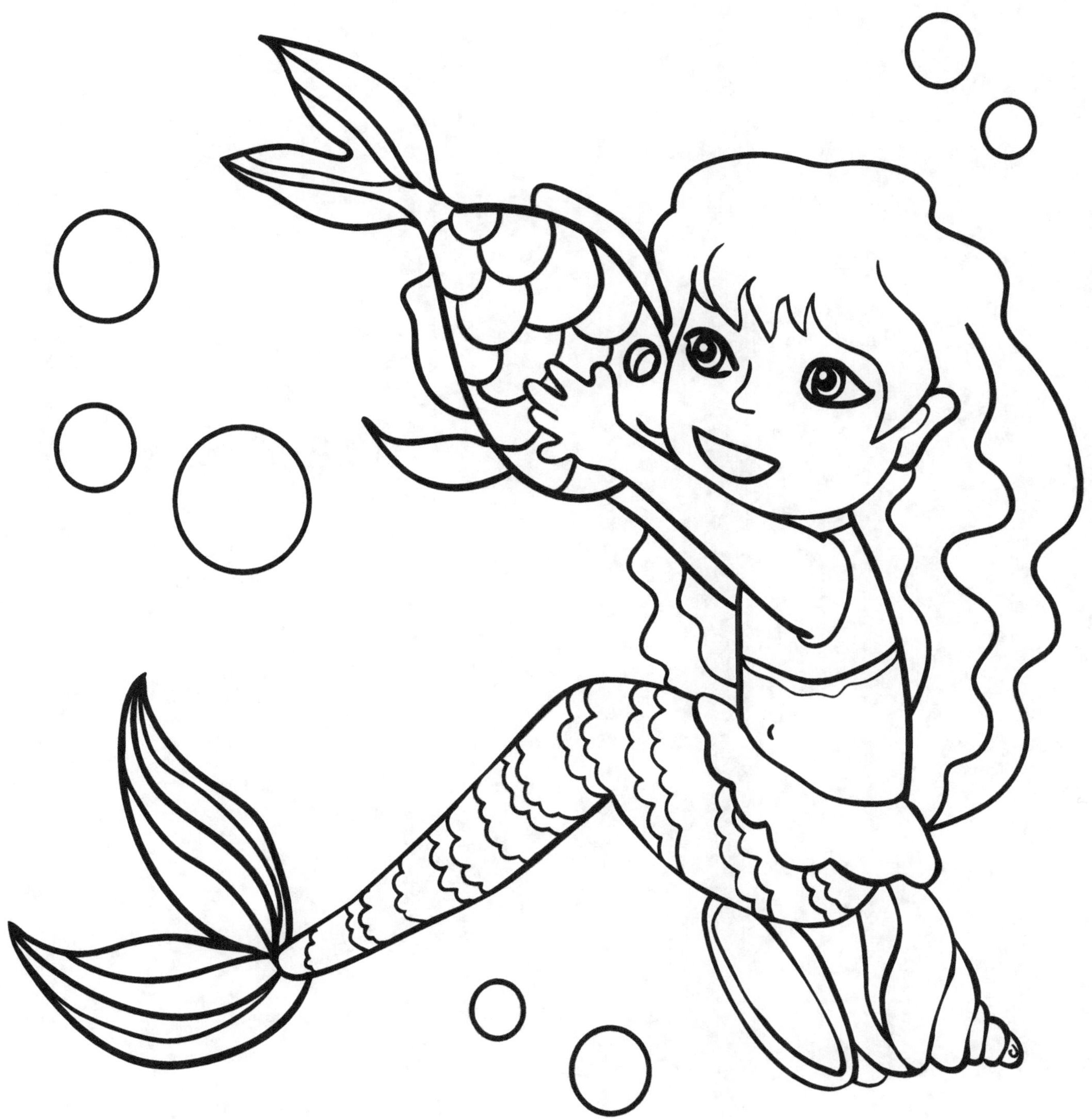

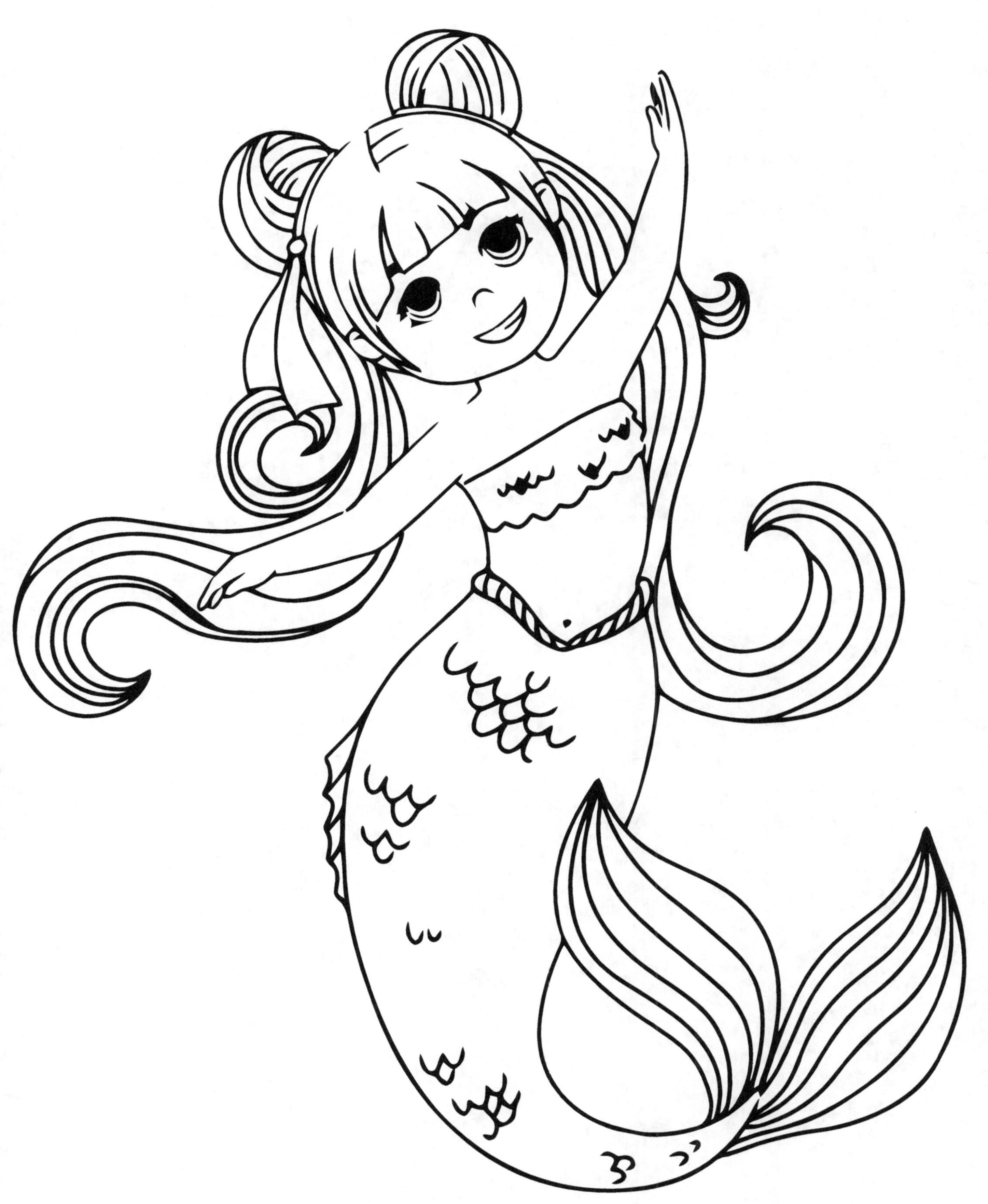

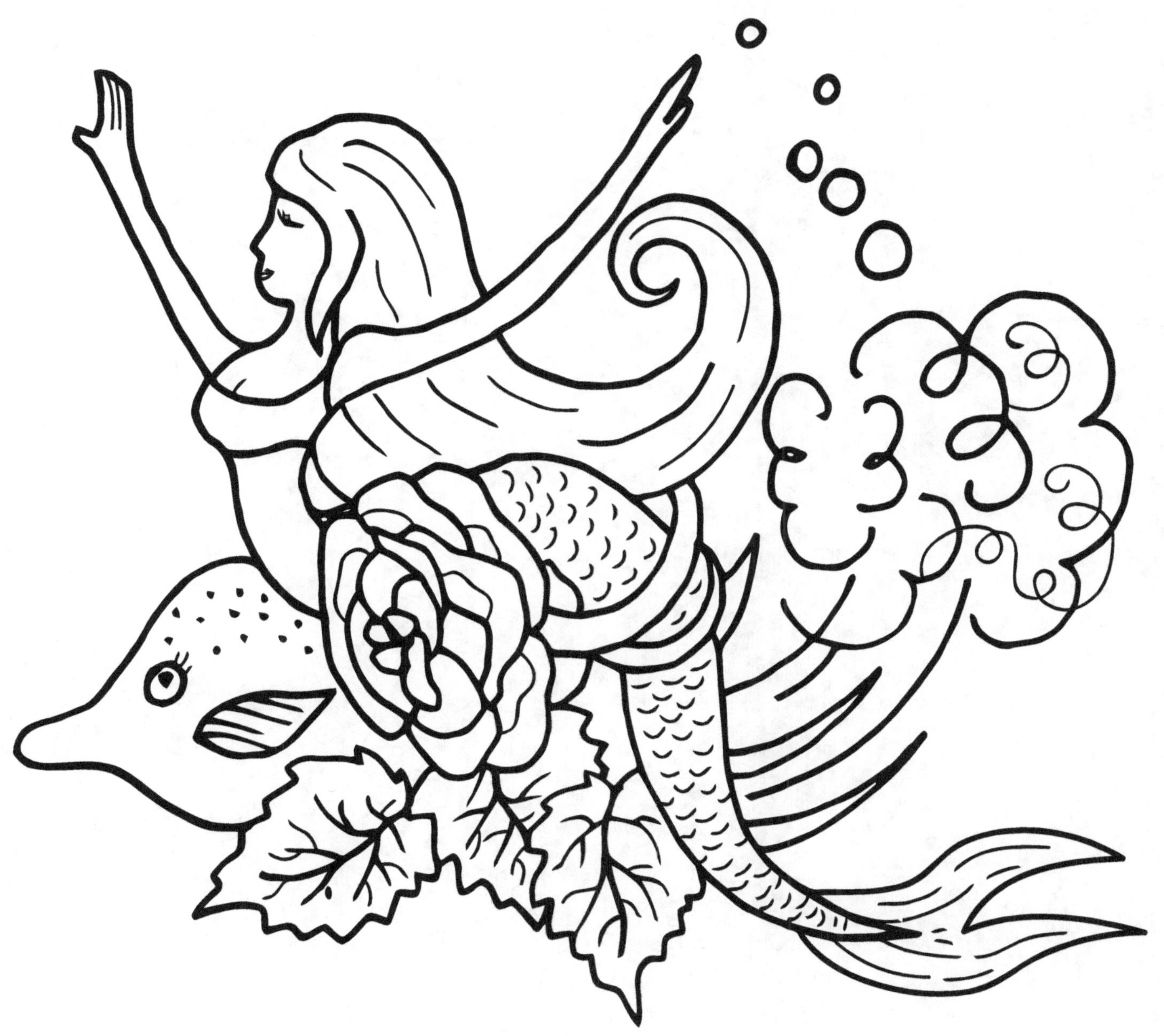

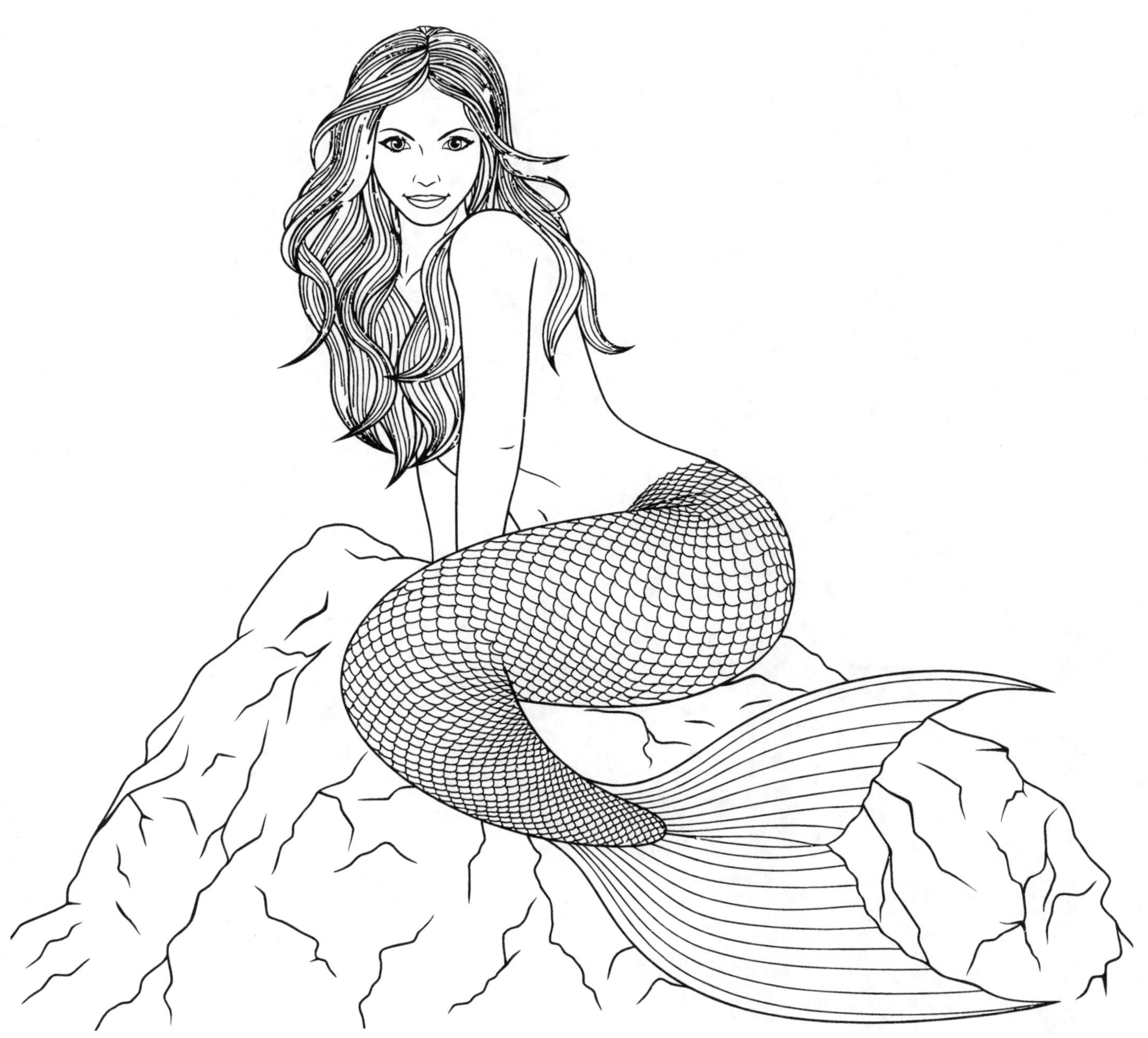

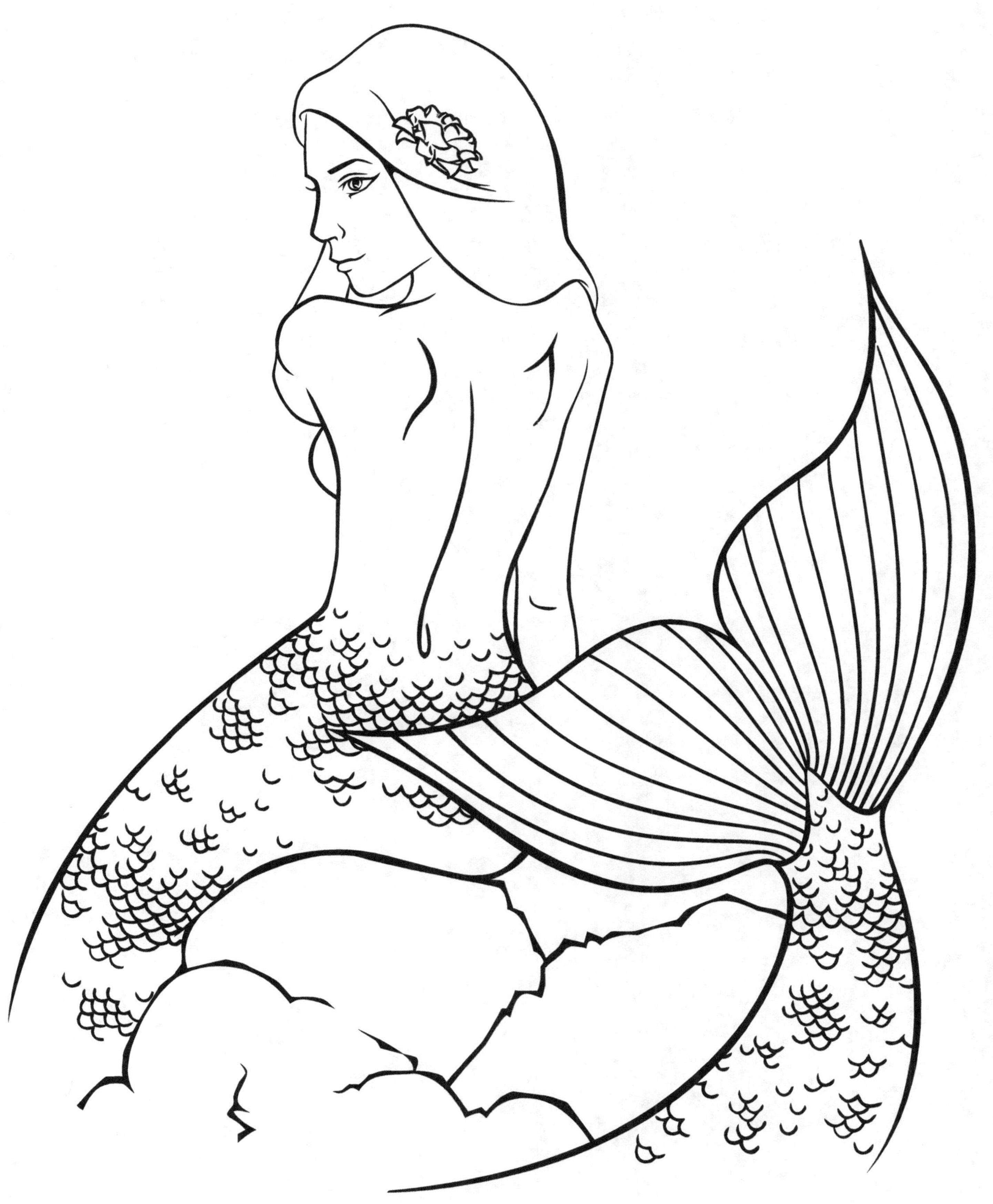

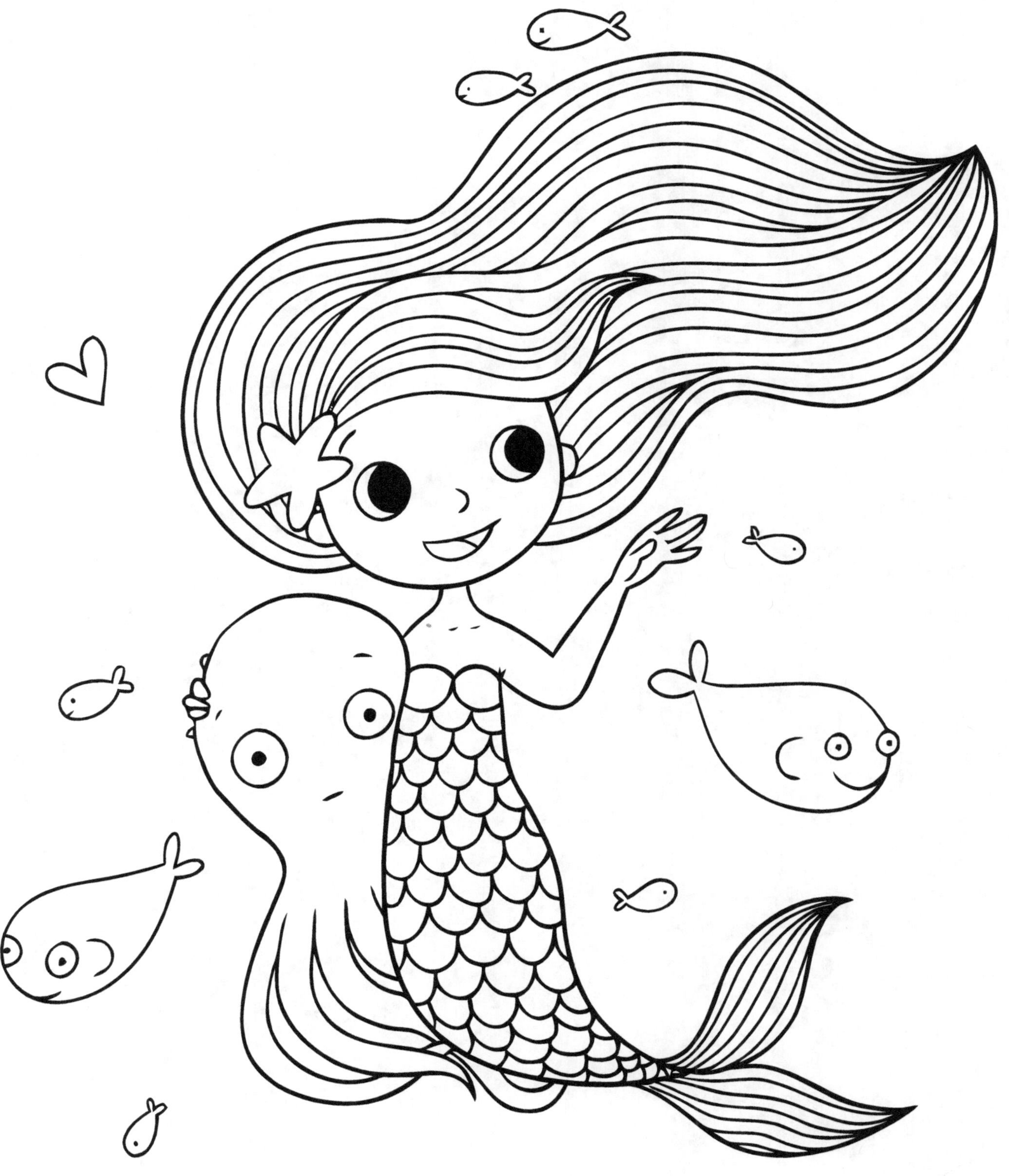

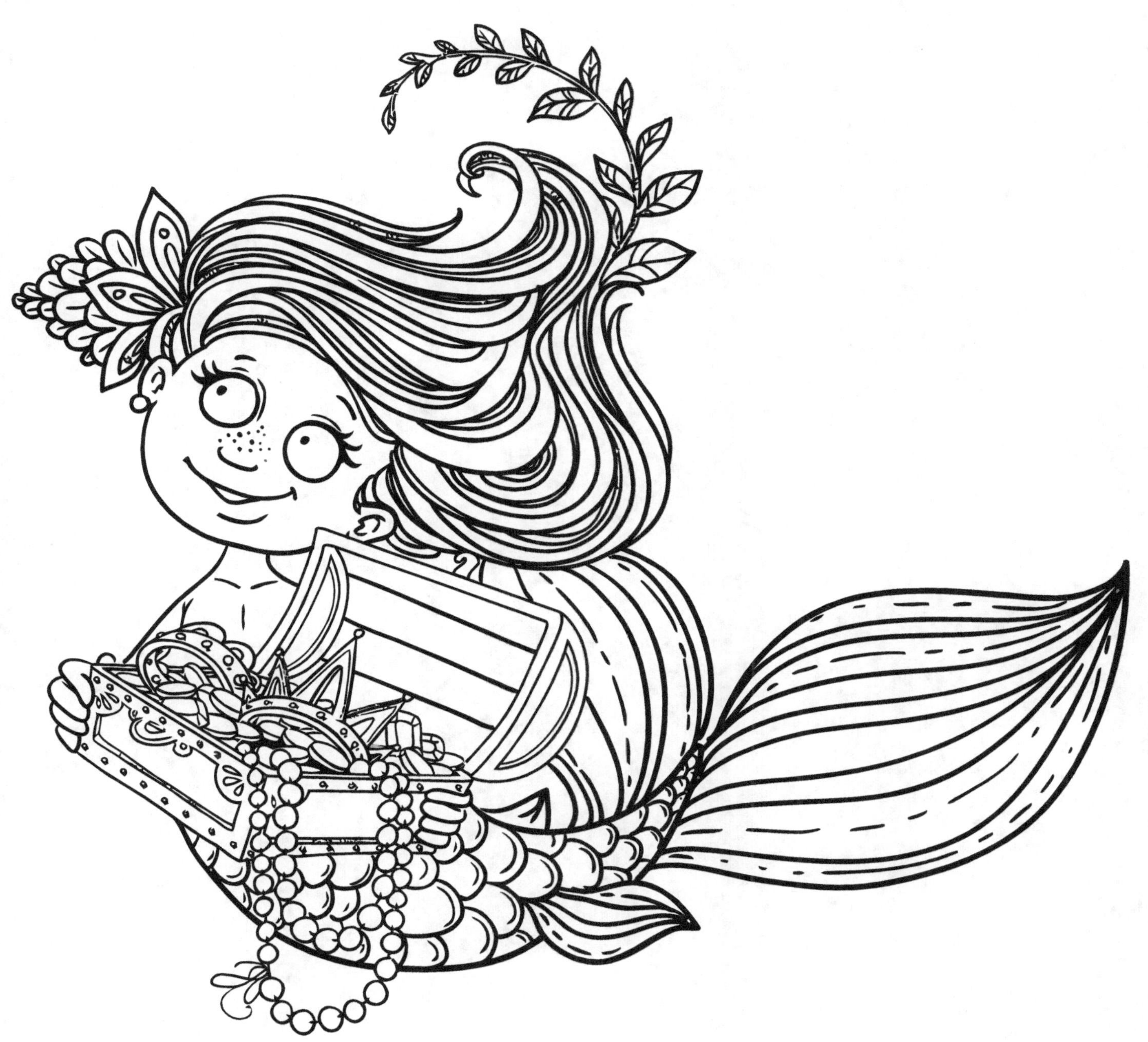

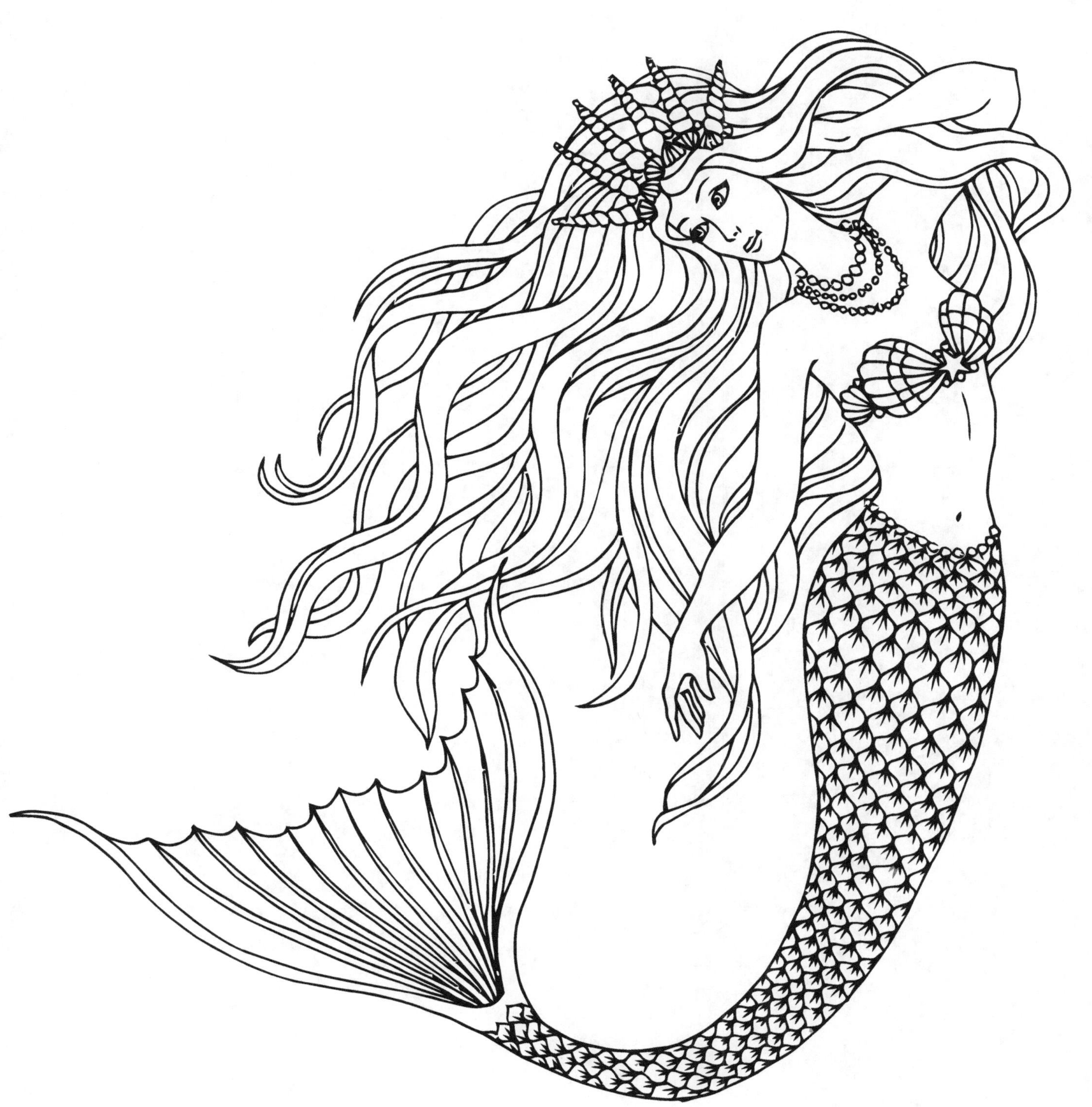

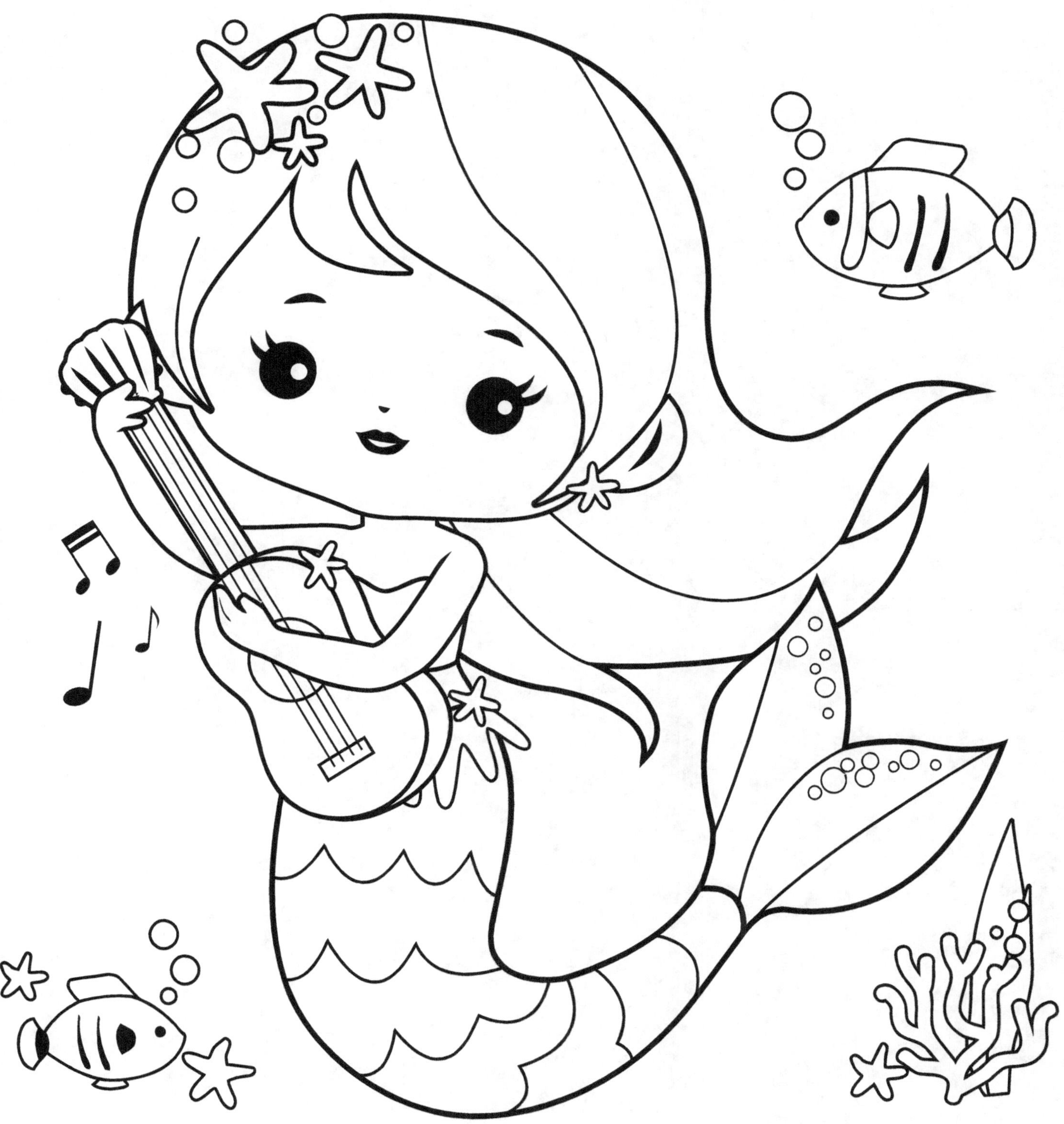

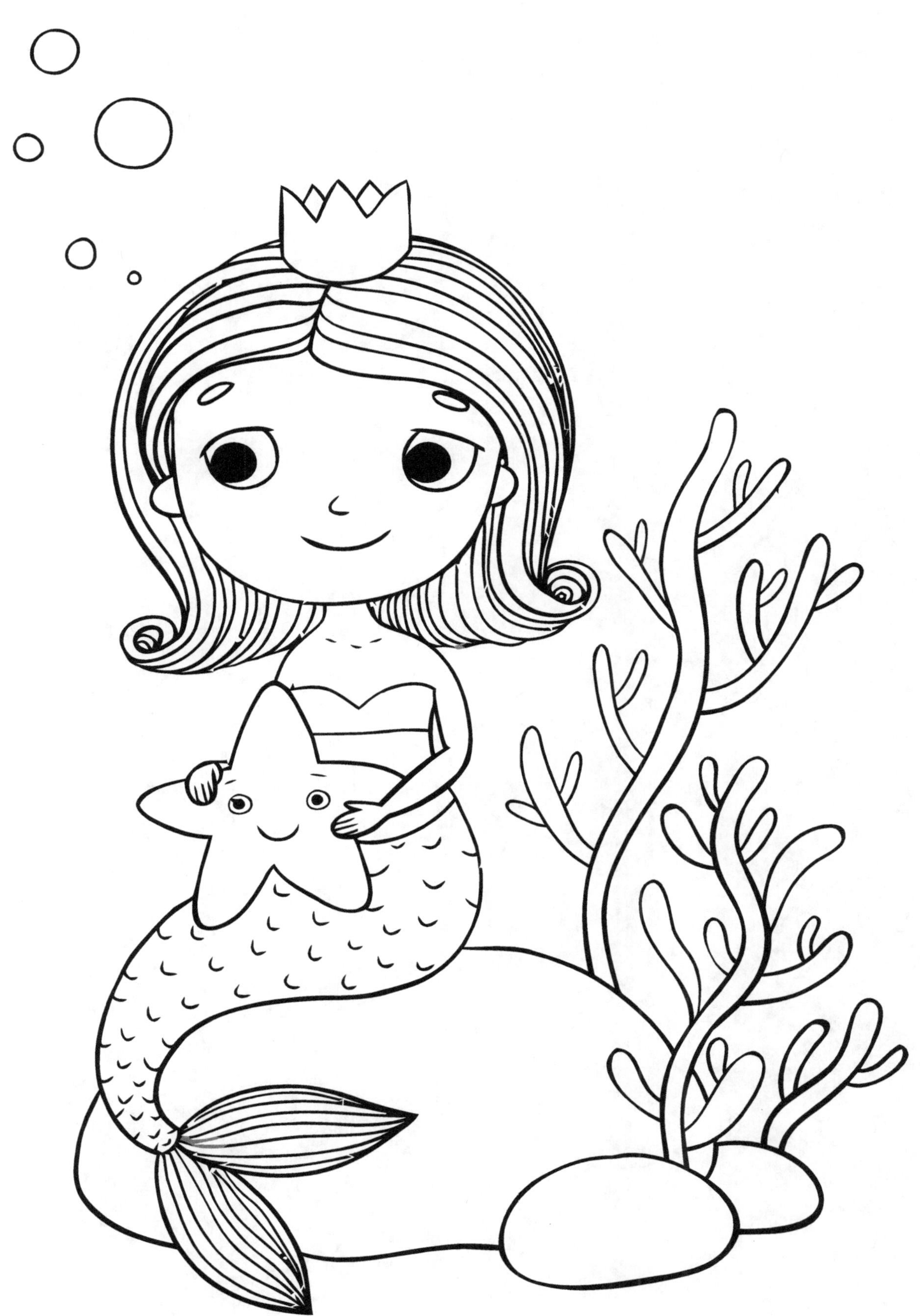

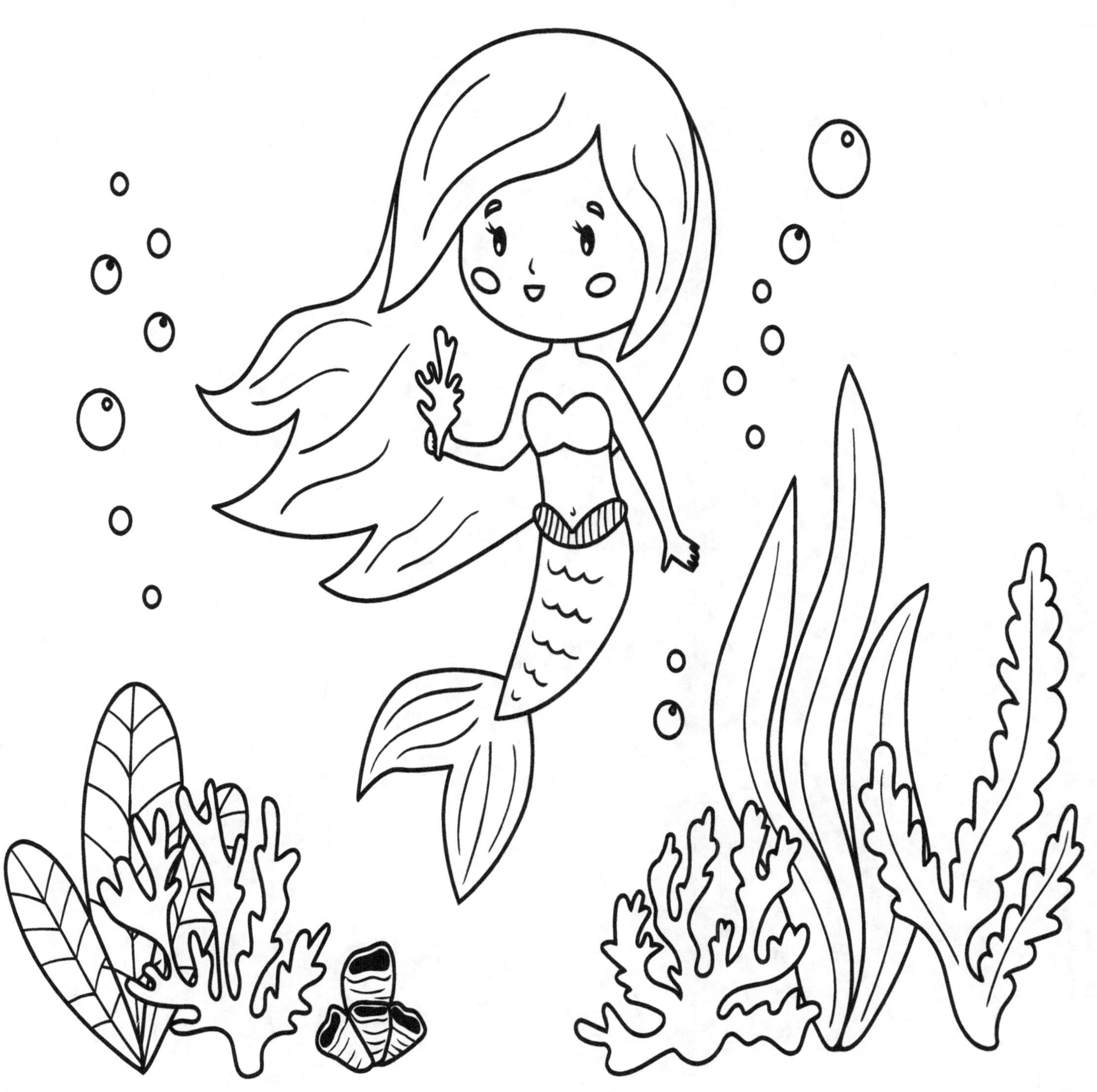

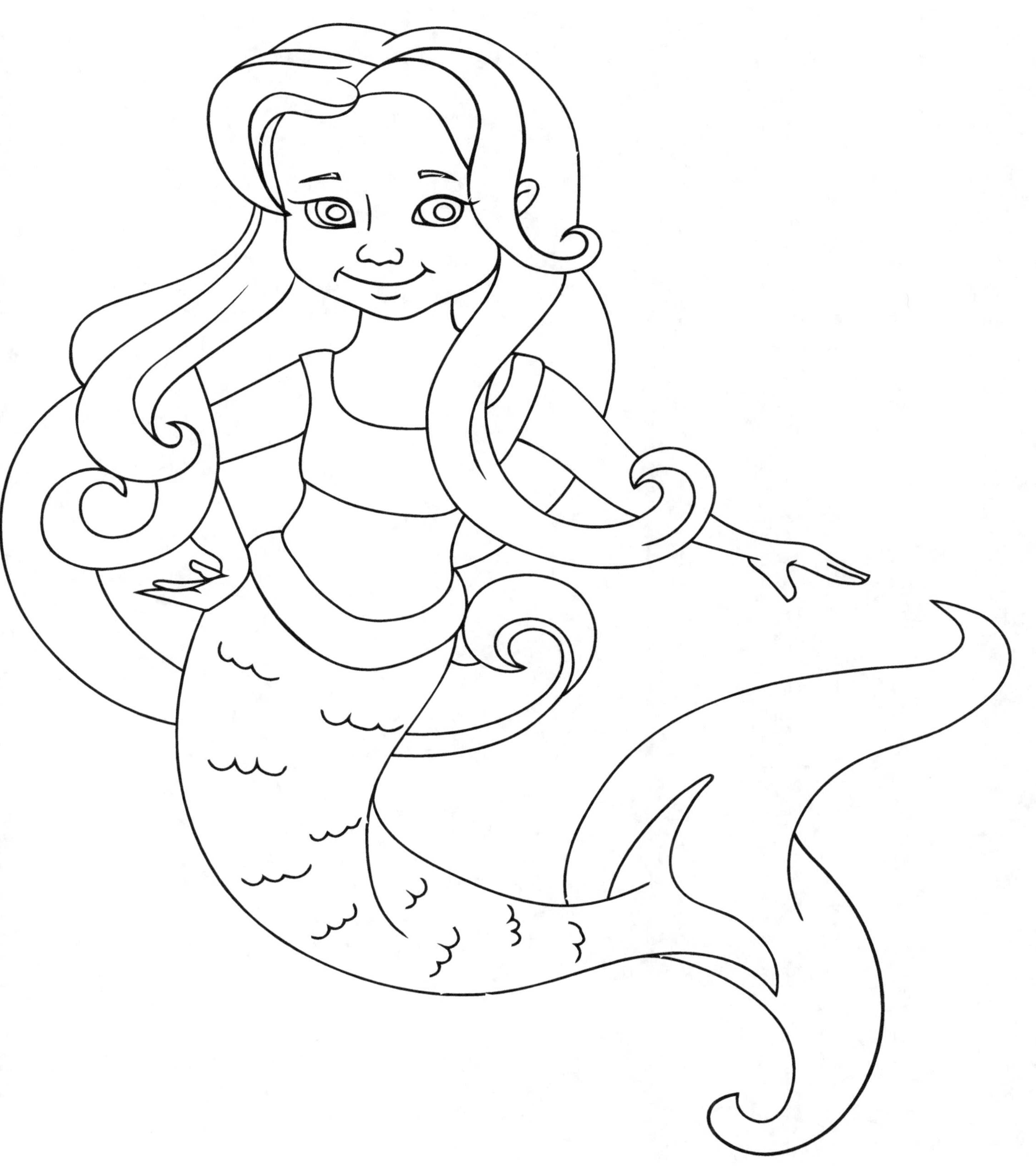

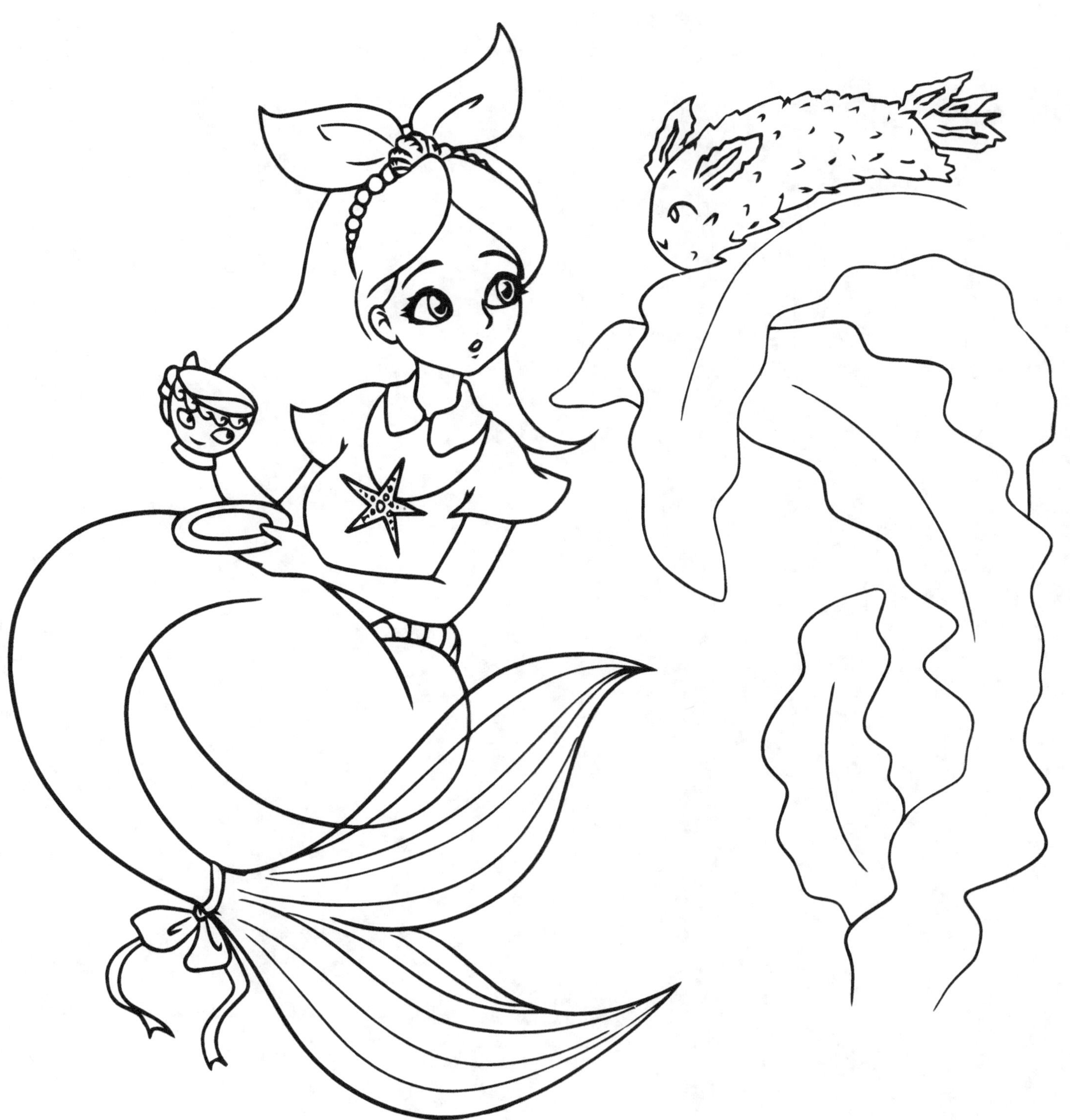

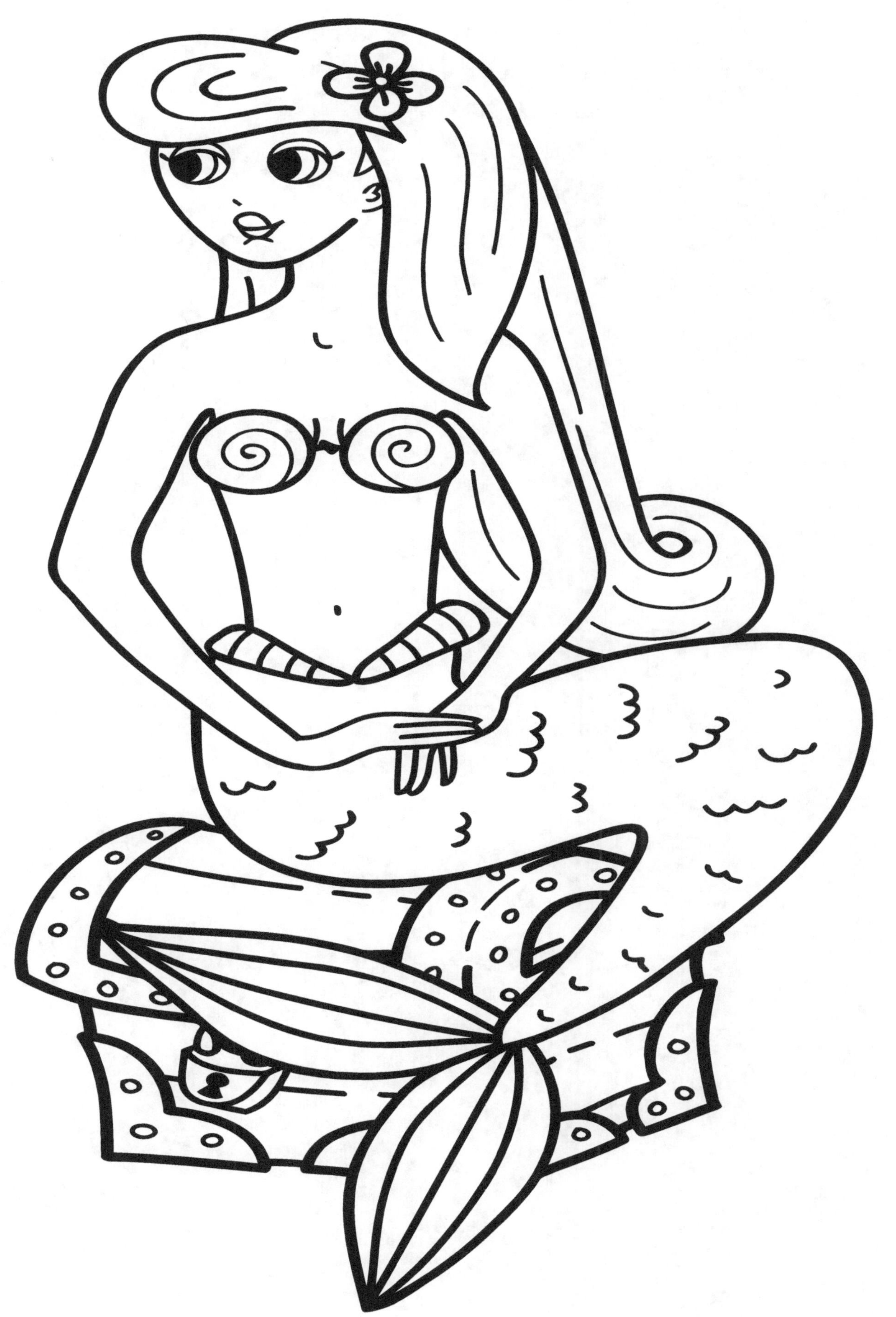

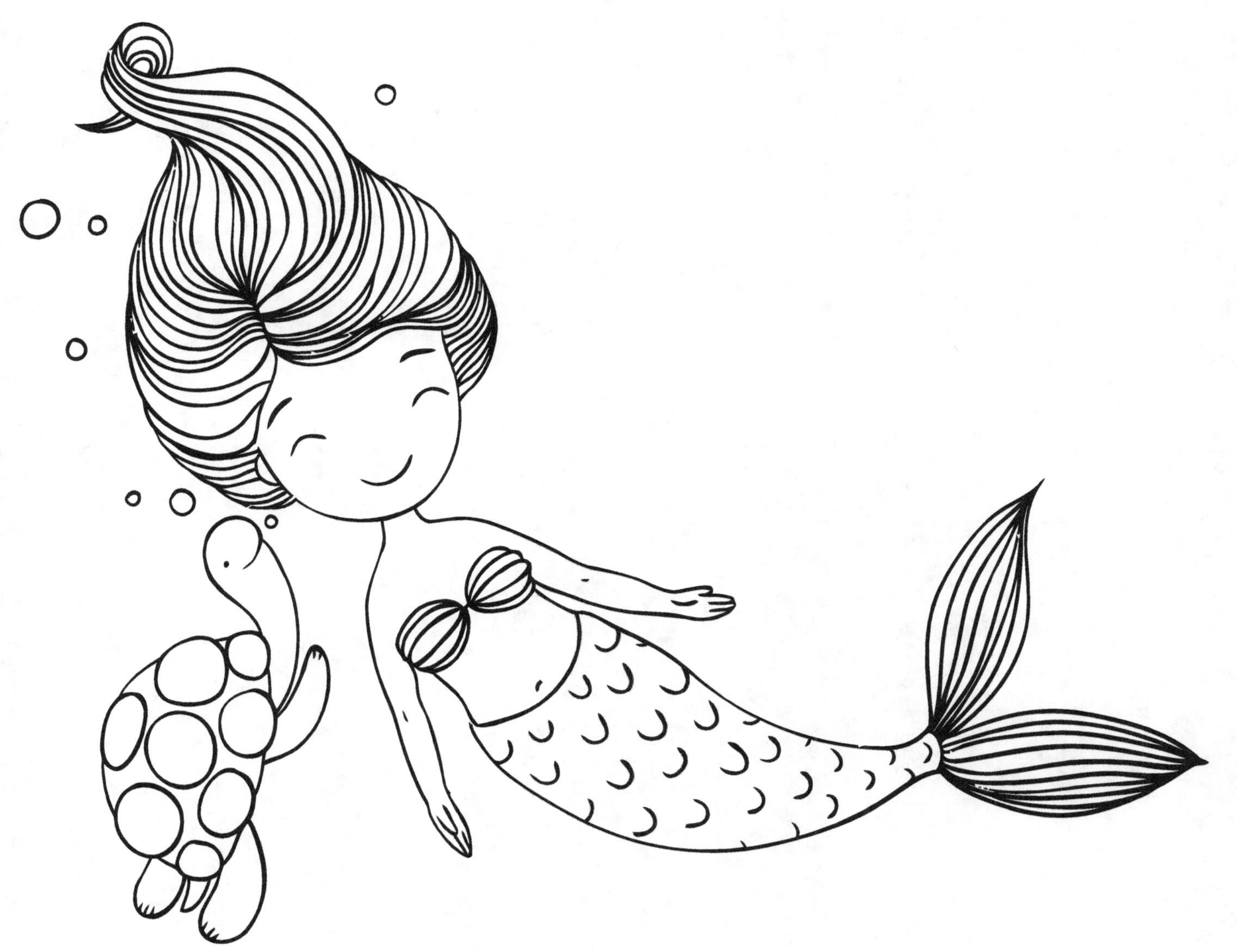

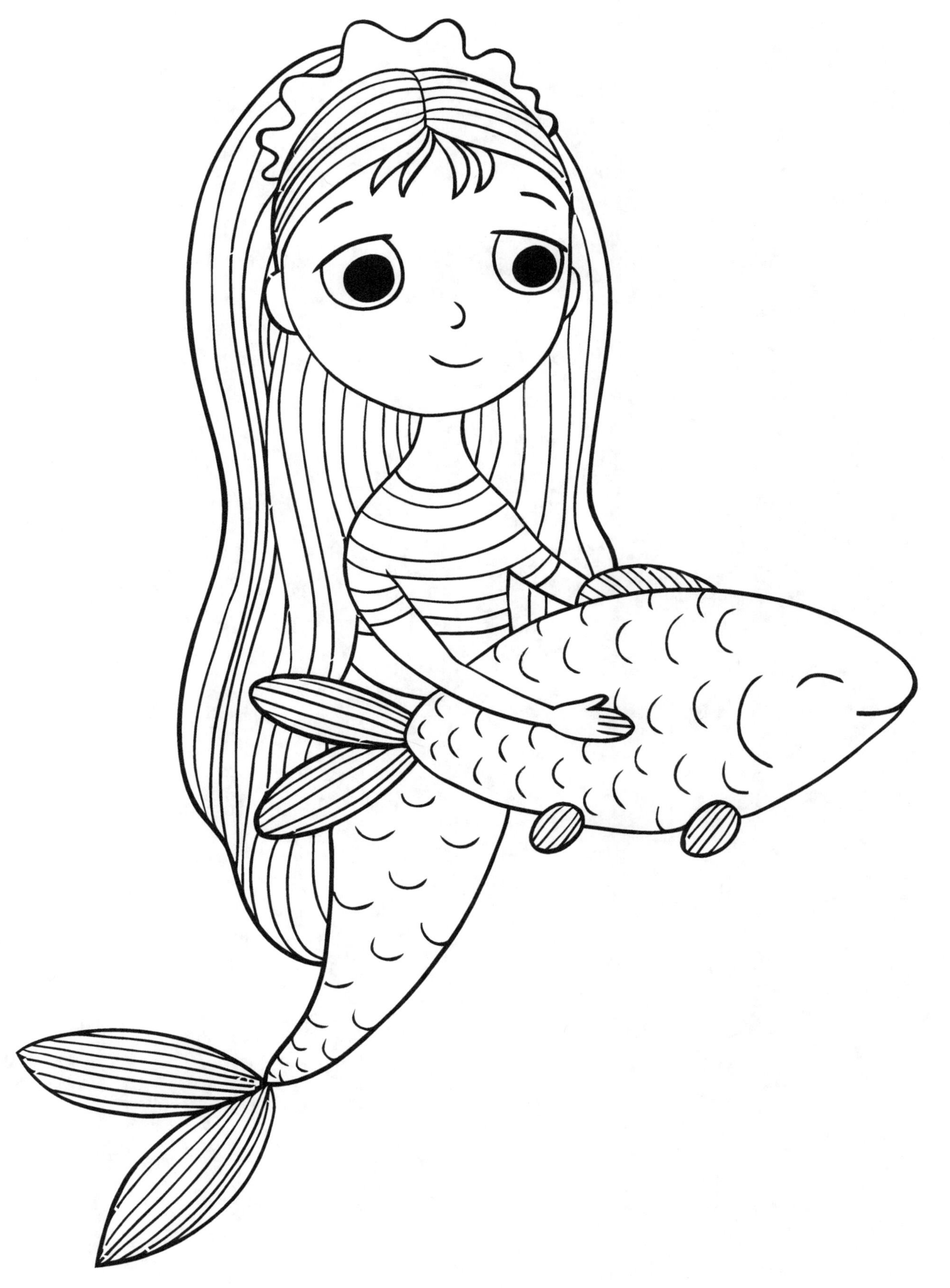